CW00369002

Paul Elvstrø EXPLAINS 1 YACHT RACING RULES

1989-92 RULES

Edited by Jonathan Bradbeer

ADLARD COLES
8 Grafton Street, London W1

Adlard Coles
William Collins Sons & Co. Ltd
8 Grafton Street, London W1X 3LA

First published in Great Britain by
Creagh Osborne & Partners Ltd December 1965
Reprinted May 1966, February 1967
Revised and reset January 1969
Reprinted June 1969, August 1971
Revised and reset April 1973
Reprinted July 1973, September 1974
Revised and reset February 1977
Revised and reset February 1981
Revised and reset edition published by Adlard Coles June 1985
Reprinted September 1985
Revised and reset 1989

British Library Cataloguing in Publication Data
Elvström, Paul
Paul Elvström explains the yacht racing rules: 1989 rules.
1. Yacht racing—Rules
I. Title   II. Bradbeer, Jonathan
797.1′4   GV826.7

ISBN 0-229-11838-0

Printed and bound in Great Britain by
BAS Printers Limited, Over Wallop, Hampshire

Wallet by Abbey Plastics Ltd, Loughton, Essex
Design by Paul Elvström and Peter Milne
Cover photograph by Alistair Black

This book contains the International Yacht Racing Rules which
come into force on 1 May 1989. The Rules are subject to change and
any clarification should be sought direct from the International
Yacht Racing Union. Whilst the Publishers and Authors have taken
care to ensure that the current Rules are stated accurately they
cannot be held responsible for any errors or changes to the Rules,
nor for their interpretation of them.

Contents Key

Rules are cross-referenced
to the Explanations and
Interpretations by RED
marginal numerals.

INTRODUCTION

The main object with *Paul Elvström Explains The Yacht Racing Rules* is to enable all of us to interpret the rules identically.

Our rules are probably the most complicated in any sport, so the best way to avoid problems is to sail against others in the same way we wish to be sailed against. This unwritten rule is the best way to preserve friendships and promote the desire to participate in yacht racing.

The rules exist in order to avoid collision, therefore it is unavoidable that one sailor must be favoured at the expense of the other. The privileged one should take this into consideration, for instance a starboard-tack yacht upwind should give sign to a port-tack yacht whether he can proceed in front or not. It is great to win in yacht racing, but only if the other competitors join in the joy. This is only possible if you always sail in a fair and gentlemanly way.

Paul Elvström

Paul Elvström. Represented Denmark at nine Olympic Games: 1948, 1952, 1956, 1960, 1964, 1968, 1972, 1984, 1988. **Olympic Champion** *1948 (Firefly), 1952, 1956 and 1960 (Finn);* **World Champion** *1957 and 1958 (505), 1958 and 1959 (Finn), 1959 (Snipe), 1962 (Flying Dutchman), 1966 (5.5), 1966 and 1967 (Star), 1969 (Soling), 1971 (¼ Ton), 1974 (Soling), 1981 (¼ Ton);* **European Champion** *1983 and 1984 (Tornado).*

How to Get the Best Use Out of This Book

The book is divided into three sections.

1. The Yacht Racing Rules as published by the IYRU.

2. A simple explanation of the various situations that can arise under each rule, in some cases supported by bird's-eye line drawings.

3. A precis of many of the Interpretations of Appeals to the IYRU together in some instances with bird's-eye line drawings.

Following an incident, look up the appropriate Rule in the BLACK section. This is a facsimile of the Rules. To avoid confusion, there is no comment in this section.

In the margin opposite the rule will be the cross reference page number printed in RED which refers you both to the Explanatory Section with RED thumb indexing and also to the relevant Interpretation Section with Red hatched thumb indexing.

The Explanatory Section is what it says – an explanation of the rule or rules involved, with line drawings to illustrate the points. To support these explanations are many of the Appeals to the IYRU. These form the Case Law for the Yacht Racing Rules and are an invaluable cross reference. It is recommended that both the serious competitor and also the student of the Rules obtains a copy of these interpretations for the full text.

In the line drawings, the red boat is either wrong, potentially wrong or in the worst position.

For quick reference, the various code flags used as signals in racing, and their meaning, are illustrated on the back cover.

I would like to thank the IYRU for their co-operation in producing this book.

Jonathan Bradbeer
January 1989

5

Summary of Changes for the 1989–92 Rules

Too many changes to a complicated rule structure can lead to unnecessary confusion for the competitors of our sport, and so it is that the Yacht Racing Rules, except for very unusual circumstances, are changed once every four years, immediately following an Olympic Games. Therefore, until after the Games in Barcelona in 1992 the rules, as now published, will remain frozen. They are effective from 1 May 1989.

During an intervening period a substantial number of alterations, deletions and additions become necessary, which are then implemented at the end of that period. The changes are to keep pace with the evolving sport of sailing; to block off loopholes, to implement new rules for new aspects of the sport or further clarification where possible. Some developments thought to be undesirable have also to be legislated for.

Here, then, is a summary of the noteworthy alterations which all racing sailors should keep abreast of.

■ There is a new Fundamental Rule D – Accepting a Penalty. This has been brought forward from Rule 33 to highlight its importance and to place greater emphasis on its compliance.

■ New Definition – Sailing. This is the first time we have seen this in the rules and it should be studied in conjunction with the rewritten Rule 54.

■ Definition of Tacking has been made much more succinct.

■ Rule 1 – The Organising, Conducting and Judging of Races has been reordered and titled. It reads much more sensibly now, and is more logical to follow.

■ Rule 13 – The Award of Prizes has been deleted and is now a spare number.

■ Rule 26 has again been completely rewritten. Events are classified in three types. Category A no advertising apart from the small makers' badges, very strictly controlled. Category B is for wide but controlled advertising on hulls, spars and sails; and note that the latter now includes fore and aft sails as well as spinnakers. Category C Special Cases which have to be cleared with the IYRU and National Authority. The details can be found in Appendix 14.

■ Rule 32 is retitled Serious Damage and now has two paragraphs: 32.1 Avoiding Collision and 32.2 Hailing, which is brought forward from Rule 34. Rule 34 is a new rule titled Maintaining Rights. This ensures that a yacht that has infringed a rule, but which continues to race, shall be granted all his rights under Part IV.

The other part of the Hailing Rule is to be found under 42.1(f) where it is felt to be more appropriate.

■ Parts of Rule 38 have been re-titled but essentially it is the same as before.

■ Rule 42 – The preamble has been sharpened up and is now easier to grasp. This is an important Rule and anything that can be done to clarify and simplify it should be welcomed. Apart from the Hailing clause already mentioned, the only other change of note is the deletion of paragraph 42.3(c) Taking an Inside Yacht to the Wrong Side of a Mark. It is felt that this is perfectly well covered by the Rule and no special clause is necessary.

■ Rule 43 – The wording is slightly changed, giving less advantage to the hailing yacht tacking on the port tack.

■ Rule 46 now includes a definition of 'capsized'.

■ One of the major alterations to the new rules lies in Rule 52.2 Touching a Mark. To exonerate oneself, having touched the mark, two 360° turns (720°) are required well clear of the mark and other competitors. The turns must include two tacks and two gybes. With that sort of penalty it behoves us all to stay clear of the mark in the future, particularly the multi-hull sailors.

■ The other big alteration is that of Rule 54; now simply called Propulsion. Something had to be done to clarify this Rule in order to avoid some of the acrimony that has surrounded the disqualifications over pumping, etc. It is much clearer now and although essentially the same rule there are two new points to note; one pump only is allowed (instead of three as before) down the front side of each wave, and in tacking the mast may not be moved away from the vertical more than once.

■ Rule 61 – organisers of offshore races no longer have to ban weight jackets specifically in their sailing instructions; reworded clause 61.4 now does that. But they must now stipulate when weight control applies 61.4.

■ Rule 64 – Setting and Sheeting Sails has been reordered and retitled and includes a clause headed Outriggers.

■ Rule 70.1 has been altered to reinforce the worries of rules compliance. This new clause enables the Race Committee to act without a hearing after Fundamental Rule C Fair Sailing and Rule 54 Propulsion have been infringed.

■ Rules 72 and 73 have had a substantial reshuffle of order and titles but essentially the wording is the same, as is the case with Rules 77 and 78.

■ Rule 75 has an added clause to enable a Race Committee to call a hearing if it believes a competitor has committed a gross infringement. It is to be much deprecated that this rule is receiving a greater usage now.

■ The Sailboard Rules in Appendix 2 have been rewritten and clarified and need careful study.

■ Appendix 4 Team Racing Rules has a section which is quite new – the Match Racing Rules. With the increase in the number of Match Racing Events this is a very welcome addition.

■ Appendix 14 is an addition. It sets out the various categories of advertising that are allowed under Rule 26.

Brief Notes of Guidance for Making a Protest

1. Following an incident you must quickly reach a decision – are you in the wrong, in which case you must either retire or accept a penalty, or are you the aggrieved yacht, in which case you must Protest (Rule 68.1). Of course, if the other yacht retires or accepts a penalty as a result of this infringement a Protest will not be necessary. But do not come ashore and grumble about the foul and fail to Protest.

2. Be sure in your mind that having decided to Protest you have (a) displayed a Protest flag at the first reasonable opportunity (Rule 68.3(b)) and (b) tried to inform the other yacht (Rule 68.2).

3. After the incident go over the events that led up to the infringement so as to be quite clear about the manner in which it happened. If it is possible, scribble some notes to remind you later about the exact details. Discuss it with your crew if you think it will help. Identify any witnesses from nearby yachts.

4. Be sure that the Race Committee acknowledges your intention to protest as you finish (Rule 68.3).

5. Once ashore you have several tasks to complete before lodging the protest:

(a) Check the latest time for lodging a Protest (Rule 68.6). It is usually two hours after Finishing but can be varied by the Sailing Instructions.

(b) Be sure you have tried to inform the Protested yacht.

(c) Contact your witnesses, if appropriate, and ask them to attend the hearing if you feel they will support your case. Make sure that your witnesses will be positive in their help. Simply padding out your case with a large number of witnesses who have little to add to the facts will do nothing but keep everybody in the Protest room longer than they wish and may alienate the Protest Committee. Do not rehearse your witness. It is usually very obvious that he has been set up in your favour and this may legislate against you.

(d) Think the incident through again. By now, you should be in a position to set out the facts, as you saw them, on the Protest Form (Rule 68.5) if one is available. If no form is supplied, any sheet of paper will do, provided it is not tatty or soggy; the Protest Committee have to read it. Do not put too much detail on the Protest Form. You can find details of what is required on page 50. A short description of the incident is all that is necessary. Add details of where and when it took place to make sure everybody knows exactly which incident you are referring to – there may have been several. And, if possible, add a note of which Rules have been infringed. A clear diagram is sometimes helpful.

(e) One final point to consider, before putting in your Protest: if the onus is on you to prove your case, and there is no positive witness in your favour and the evidence is poor, think very carefully before lodging the Protest. You have to have a very good case, otherwise it is a lost cause. Such circumstances are:

(i) An outside yacht has to satisfy the Protest Committee that she was clear ahead at the moment she reached the two *yacht* length circle around a mark (Rule 42.1(c)).

(ii) An inside yacht has to satisfy the Protest Committee that she established her overlap in time (Rule 42.1(d)).

(iii) A tacking or gybing yacht must satisfy the Protest Committee that she does so in accordance with Rule 41.2 (Rule 41.3).

6. Now lodge the Protest (you may be required to include a fee (Rule 68.7)). No action can be taken by the Protest Committee to hear your Protest unless you lodge it within the required time limit. Remember, once you have lodged a Protest it must be heard, with one exception – see Rule 68.9.

7. Make sure you know where and when your Protest is to be heard. The Sailing Instructions should detail where the notice will be posted.

8. During the hearing, which should follow the procedure set out in Appendix 6, treat the Protest Committee with respect. They will almost certainly be yachtsmen like yourself doing their best for everybody concerned. Do not be rude or lose your temper – it will do nothing to further your case.

9. In establishing your case it is often helpful to work back from the incident. The facts as you see them will come out during the hearing. The following table of Rate of Advance of a yacht may be helpful in establishing distances.

1kt = .51 m/sec
2kt = 1.03 m/sec
3kt = 1.54 m/sec
4kt = 2.11 m/sec
5kt = 2.57 m/sec
6kt = 3.09 m/sec
7kt = 3.60 m/sec
8kt = 4.12 m/sec
9kt = 4.63 m/sec
10kt = 5.14 m/sec

10. Remember there is no substitute for care in the preparation of your case.

11. A point for Protest Committees – it is very helpful to the competitor if, when you announce your verdict, you give some background to your decision. Not only will the competitor learn from that, but it will go a long way towards maintaining the good spirit of the Event.

THE 1989-92 INTERNATIONAL YACHT RACING RULES

Introduction

Translation and Interpretation
In translating and interpreting these rules, it shall be understood that the word "shall" is mandatory, and the words "can" and "may" are permissive.

Notes: (a) These rules become effective on May 1, 1989.

(b) Marginal markings indicate the changes made in the 1985 Racing Rules.

(c) No changes are contemplated before 1993.

(d) These rules supersede all previous editions.

CONTENTS

Contents

IYRU Rules

Contents

APPENDICES

Part I—Status of the Rules, Fundamental Rules and Definitions

Status of the Rules

The International Yacht Racing Rules have been established by the International Yacht Racing Union for the organisation, conduct and judging of the sport of yacht racing, and are amended and published every four years by the IYRU in accordance with its Constitution.

A national authority may alter or add to these rules by prescription, with the exception of the rules of Parts I and IV, the definitions of Part VI, rules 1, 3, 26 and 61, and Appendix 14, unless permitted in a rule itself.

The sailing instructions may alter rules only in accordance with rule 3.1, Sailing Instructions.

Fundamental Rules

A. Rendering Assistance

107

Every yacht shall render all possible assistance to any vessel or person in peril, when in a position to do so.

B. Responsibility of a Yacht

107

It shall be the sole responsibility of each yacht to decide whether or not to *start* or to continue to *race*.

C. Fair Sailing

107

A yacht, her owner and crew shall compete only by *sailing*, using their speed and skill, and, except in team racing, by individual effort, in compliance with the **rules** and in accordance with recognised principles of fair play and sportsmanship. A yacht may be penalised under this rule only in the case of a clear-cut violation of the above principles and only when no other **rule** applies, except rule 75, Gross Infringement of Rules or Misconduct.

D. Accepting Penalties

107

A yacht that realises she has infringed a **rule** shall either retire promptly or accept an alternative penalty when so prescribed in the sailing instructions.

Definitions

When a term defined in Part I is used in its defined sense it is printed in italic type. All preambles and definitions rank as rules. Further definitions will be found at the beginning of Part VI.

Sailing - A yacht is *sailing* when using only the wind and water to increase, maintain

Definitions

or decrease her speed, with her crew adjusting the trim of sails and hull and performing other acts of seamanship.

Racing - A yacht is *racing* from her preparatory signal until she has either *finished* and cleared the finishing line and finishing *marks* or retired, or until the race has been *postponed, abandoned, cancelled,* or a general recall has been signalled.

Starting - A yacht *starts* when, after fulfilling her penalty obligations, if any, under rule 51.1(c), Sailing the Course, and after her starting signal, any part of her hull, crew or equipment first crosses the starting line in the direction of the course to the first *mark*.

Finishing - A yacht *finishes* when any part of her hull, or of her crew or equipment in normal position, crosses the finishing line in the direction of the course from the last *mark*, after fulfilling her penalty obligations, if any, under rule 52.2(b), Touching a Mark.

Luffing - Altering course towards the wind.

Tacking - A yacht is *tacking* from the moment she is beyond head to wind until she has *borne away* to a *close-hauled* course.

Bearing away - Altering course away from the wind until a yacht begins to *gybe*.

Gybing - A yacht begins to *gybe* at the moment when, with the wind aft, the foot of her mainsail crosses her centre line, and completes the *gybe* when the mainsail has filled on the other *tack*.

On a tack - A yacht is *on a tack* except when she is *tacking* or *gybing*. A yacht is on the *tack (starboard* or *port)* corresponding to her *windward* side.

Close-hauled - A yacht is *close-hauled* when *sailing* by the wind as close as she can lie with advantage in working to windward.

Clear Astern and *Clear Ahead; Overlap* - A yacht is *clear astern* of another when her hull and equipment in normal position are abaft an imaginary line projected abeam from the aftermost point of the other's hull and equipment in normal position. The other yacht is *clear ahead*.

The yachts *overlap* when neither is *clear astern;* or when, although one is *clear astern*, an intervening yacht *overlaps* both of them.

The terms *clear astern, clear ahead* and *overlap* apply to yachts on opposite *tacks* only when they are subject to rule 42, Rounding or Passing Marks and Obstructions.

Leeward and Windward - The *leeward* side of a yacht is that on which she is, or, when head to wind, was, carrying her mainsail. The opposite side is the *windward* side.

When neither of two yachts on the same *tack* is *clear astern*, the one on the *leeward* side of the other is the *leeward yacht*. The other is the *windward yacht*.

Proper Course - A *proper course* is any course that a yacht might *sail* after the starting signal, in the absence of the other yacht or yachts affected, to *finish* as quickly as possible. The course *sailed* before *luffing* or *bearing away* is presumably, but not necessarily, that yacht's *proper course*. There is no *proper course* before the starting signal.

Mark - A *mark* is any object specified in the sailing instructions that a yacht must round or pass on a required side.

Every ordinary part of a *mark* ranks as part of it, including a flag, flagpole, boom or hoisted boat, but excluding ground tackle and any object either accidentally or temporarily attached to the *mark*.

Obstruction - An *obstruction* is any object, including a vessel under way, large enough to require a yacht, when more than one overall length away from it, to make a substantial alteration of course to pass on one side or the other, or any object that can be passed on one side only, including a buoy when the yacht in question cannot safely pass between it and the shoal or object that it marks. The sailing instructions may prescribe that certain defined areas shall rank as *obstructions*.

Postponement - A *postponed* race is one that is not started at its scheduled time and that can be sailed at any time the race committee may decide.

Abandonment - An *abandoned* race is one that the race committee declares void at any time after the starting signal, and that can be re-sailed at its discretion.

Cancellation - A *cancelled* race is one that the race committee decides will not be sailed thereafter.

Part II—**Organisation and Management**

1   Organising, Conducting and Judging Races

1.1   GOVERNING RULES

The organising authority, race committee, protest committee and all other bodies and persons concerned with the organisation, conduct and judging of a race, regatta or series shall be governed by these rules, the prescriptions of the national authority when they apply, the class rules (except when they conflict with these rules), the sailing instructions and any other conditions governing the event. Hereinafter the term 'race' shall, when appropriate, include a regatta or a series of races.

1.2   ORGANISING AUTHORITY

Races shall be organised by:

(a)   the IYRU; or

(b)   a member national authority of the IYRU; or

(c)   a club or regatta committee affiliated to a national authority; or

(d)   a class association either with the approval of a national authority or in conjunction with an affiliated club or regatta committee; or

(e)   an unaffiliated body in conjunction with an affiliated club or regatta committee;

which will hereinafter be referred to as the organising authority.

The organising authority shall appoint a race committee and publish a notice of race in accordance with rule 2, Notice of Race.

1.3   RACE COMMITTEE

The race committee shall publish sailing instructions in accordance with rule 3, Sailing Instructions, and conduct the race, subject to such direction as the organising authority may exercise. The term "race committee" whenever it is used shall include any person or committee that is responsible for performing any of the duties or functions of the race committee.

1.4   PROTEST COMMITTEES

The receiving, hearing, and deciding of protests and other matters arising under the rules of Part VI, Protests, Penalties and Appeals, shall be carried out by:

(a)   the race committee itself; or

(b)   a sub-committee thereof appointed by the race committee and consisting of its own members, or others, or a combination of both; or

(c)   a jury or a protest committee, separate from and independent of the race committee, appointed by the organising authority or the race committee; or

(d)   an international jury appointed by the organising authority in accordance with Appendix 8, International Juries. A national authority may prescribe that its approval is required for the appointment of international juries for events within its jurisdiction other than those of the IYRU.

A jury or protest committee shall not supervise the conduct of the race, or direct the race committee, except when so directed by the organising authority. (The term "jury", as used in yacht racing, means a panel of judges.)

1.5   RIGHT OF APPEAL
Decisions of a **protest committee** may be appealed in accordance with rule 77.1, Right of Appeal, except that:

(a)   there shall be no appeal from the decisions of an international jury constituted in accordance with Appendix 8, International Juries.

(b)   when the notice of race and the sailing instructions so state, the right of appeal may be denied when:

(i)   it is essential to determine promptly the result of a race that will qualify a yacht to compete in a later stage of the event or a subsequent event (a national authority may prescribe that its approval is required for such a procedure); or

(ii)   a national authority so prescribes for a particular event open only to entrants under its own jurisdiction.

1.6   EXCLUSION OF YACHTS AND COMPETITORS
Unless otherwise prescribed by the national authority, the organising authority or the race committee may, before the start of the first race, reject or rescind the entry of any yacht or exclude a competitor, without stating the reason. However, at all world and continental championships, no entry within established quotas shall be rejected or rescinded without first obtaining the approval of the IYRU, the relevant international class association or the Offshore Racing Council.

2   **Notice of Race**

The notice of race shall contain the following information:

(a)   The title, place and dates of the event and name of the organising authority.

(b)   That the race will be governed by the International Yacht Racing Rules, the prescriptions of the national authority when they apply (for international events, a copy in English of prescriptions that apply shall be available to each yacht), the rules of each class concerned, and such other rules as are applicable. When class rules are altered, the alterations shall be stated.

(c)   The class(es) to *race*, conditions of eligibility or entry and, when appropriate, restrictions on numbers of entries.

(d)   The times of registration and starts of the practice race or first race, and succeeding races when known.

The notice shall, when appropriate, include the following:

(e)   The category of the event in accordance with Appendix 14, Event

Classification and Advertising, and, when required, the additional
information prescribed in Appendix 14.

(f) The scoring system.

(g) The time and place at which the sailing instructions will be available.

(h) Variations from the racing rules, subject to rule 3.1, Sailing Instructions.

(i) The procedure for advance registration or entry, including closing dates
when applicable, fees and the mailing address.

(j) Measurement procedures or requirements for measuring or rating
certificates.

(k) The course(s) to be *sailed*.

(l) Alternative penalties for rule infringements.

(m) Prizes.

(n) Denial of the right of appeal, subject to rule 1.5, Right of Appeal.

3   Sailing Instructions

3.1   STATUS

(a) These rules shall be supplemented by written sailing instructions that
shall rank as rules and may, subject to the restrictions of rule 3.1(b),
alter a rule by specific reference to it.

(b) Except in accordance with rule 3.2(b) (xxix), the sailing instructions
shall not alter:

   (i)   Parts I and IV,

   (ii)   rules 1, 2, 3, 26, 51.1(a) and 61,

   (iii) the definitions and Sections C and D of Part VI,

   (iv)   Appendix 14, and

   (v)   the provision of rule 68.3(a), Protests by Yachts, that
International Code flag "B" is always acceptable as a protest
flag.

(c) When so prescribed by the national authority, these restrictions shall
not preclude the right of developing and testing proposed rule changes
in local races. A national authority may also prescribe that its approval
is required for such changes.

3.2   CONTENTS

(a) The sailing instructions shall contain the following information:

   (i)   That the race will be governed by the International Yacht
Racing Rules, the prescriptions of the national authority when
they apply (for international events, a copy in English of
prescriptions that apply shall be included in the sailing
instructions), the rules of each class concerned, the sailing
instructions and such other rules as are applicable.

   (ii)   The schedule of races, the classes to *race*, and the order and
times of warning signals.

116

(iii) The course to be *sailed* or a list of *marks* from which the course will be selected, describing the *marks*, stating their order and, for each, whether it is to be rounded or passed and on which side.

A diagram or chart is recommended.

(iv) Description of the starting line, the starting system and any special signals to be used.

(v) The procedure for individual and general recalls and any special signals.

(vi) Description of the finishing line and any special instructions for *finishing* a course shortened after the start.

(vii) The time limit, if any, for *finishing*.

(viii) The scoring system, when not previously announced in writing, including the method, if any, for breaking ties.

(b) The sailing instructions shall, when appropriate, include the following:

(i) The category of the event in accordance with Appendix 14, Event Classification and Advertising, and, when required, the additional information prescribed in Appendix 14.

(ii) Variations from the racing rules, subject to rule 3.1, or the class rules for a special race.

(iii) The registration procedure.

(iv) Location(s) of official notice board(s).

(v) Procedure for changes in the sailing instructions.

(vi) Restrictions controlling alterations to yachts when supplied by the organising authority.

(vii) Signals to be made ashore and location of signal station(s).

(viii) Class flags.

(ix) The racing area. A chart is recommended.

(x) The starting area.

(xi) Course signals.

(xii) Approximate course length; approximate length of windward legs.

(xiii) Information on tides and currents.

(xiv) Procedure for shortening the course before or after the start.

(xv) Mark boats; lead boats.

(xvi) Procedure for changes of course after the start and related signals.

(xvii) The time limit, if any, for yachts other than the first yacht to *finish*.

(xviii) Whether races *postponed* or *abandoned* for the day will be sailed later and, if so, when and where.

(xix)   The number of races required to complete the regatta.

(xx)   Safety, such as requirements and signals for personal buoyancy, check-in at the starting area, and check-out and check-in ashore.

(xxi)   Any measurement or inspection procedure.

(xxii)   Alternative penalties for rule infringements.

(xxiii)   Whether declarations are required.

(xxiv)   Protest procedure and times and place of hearings.

(xxv)   Restrictions on use of support boats, plastic pools, radios, etc., and limitations on hauling out.

(xxvi)   Substitute competitors.

(xxvii)   Prizes.

(xxviii)   Time allowances.

(xxix)   Racing rules applicable between sunset and sunrise and night signals to be used by the race committee.

(xxx)   Disposition to be made of a yacht appearing at the start alone in her class.

(xxxi)   Denial of the right of appeal, subject to rule 1.5, Right of Appeal.

(xxxii)   Other commitments of the race committee and obligations of yachts.

3.3 DISTRIBUTION

The sailing instructions shall be available to each yacht entitled to *race*.

3.4 CHANGES

Changes in sailing instructions shall be made in writing before a race by:

(a)   posting in proper time on the official notice board, or

(b)   being communicated to each yacht on the water before the warning signal, except that oral instructions may be given only on the water in accordance with procedure prescribed in the sailing instructions.

117

4   Signals

4.1 VISUAL SIGNALS

Unless otherwise prescribed in the sailing instructions, the following International Code flags (or boards) and other visual signals shall be used as indicated, and when displayed alone shall apply to all classes, and when displayed over a class flag shall apply to the designated class only:

"AP", Answering Pendant - Postponement Signal

Means:

(a)   "All races not started are *postponed*. The warning signal will be made one minute after this signal is lowered."
(One sound signal shall be made with the lowering of the "AP".)

(b) Over one ball or shape.

"The scheduled starting times of all races not started are *postponed* fifteen minutes."
(This *postponement* can be extended indefinitely by the addition of one ball or shape for every fifteen minutes.)

(c) Over one of the numeral pendants 1 to 9.
"All races not started are *postponed* one hour, two hours, etc."

(d) Over Code flag "A".
"All races not started are *postponed* to a later day."

"B" — Protest signal.

When displayed by a yacht, means:
"I intend to lodge a **protest.**"

"C" — Change of Course while Racing.

When displayed at or near a rounding *mark*, means:
"After rounding this *mark*, the course to the next *mark* has been changed."

"I" —   Round the Ends Starting Rule

When displayed before or with the preparatory signal, means:
"Rule 51.1(c) will be in effect for this start."

When lowered, accompanied by one long sound signal, one minute before the starting signal, means:
"The one-minute period of rule 51.1(c) has begun."

"L" — Means:

(a) When displayed ashore:
"A notice to competitors has been posted on the official notice board."

(b) When displayed afloat:
"Come within hail", or "Follow me".

"M" — Mark Signal.

When displayed on a buoy, vessel, or other object, means:
"Round or pass the object displaying this signal instead of the *mark* that it replaces."

"N" — Abandonment Signal.

Means:
"All races are *abandoned*."

"N over X" —Abandonment and Re-sail Signal.

Means:
"All races are *abandoned* and will shortly be re-sailed. The warning signal will be made one minute after this signal is lowered."
(One sound signal shall be made with the lowering of "N over X".)

"N over First Substitute" —Cancellation Signal.

Means:
"All races are *cancelled*."

"P" — Preparatory Signal.

Means:
"The class designated by the warning signal will *start* in five minutes exactly."

"S" — Shorten Course Signal.

Means:
(a) at the starting line:
"*Sail* the shortened course as prescribed in the sailing instructions."

(b) at the finishing line:
"*Finish* the race either:
(i) at the prescribed finishing line at the end of the round still to be completed by the leading yacht, or
(ii) as prescribed in the sailing instructions."

(c) at a rounding *mark*:
"*Finish* between the rounding *mark* and the committee boat."

"X" — Individual Recall.

When displayed promptly after the starting signal, accompanied by one sound signal, means:
"One or more yachts are recalled in accordance with rule 8.1, Individual Recall."

"Y" — Life Jacket Signal.
Means:
"Life jackets or other adequate personal buoyancy shall be worn while *racing* by all competitors, unless specifically excepted in the sailing instructions."
When this signal is displayed after the warning signal, failure to comply shall not be cause for disqualification.
Notwithstanding anything in this rule, it shall be the individual responsibility of each competitor to wear a life jacket or other adequate personal buoyancy when conditions warrant. A wet suit is not adequate personal buoyancy.

"First Substitute" —General Recall Signal.

Means:
"The class is recalled for a new start. The preparatory signal will be made one minute after this signal is lowered."
(One sound signal shall be made with the lowering of "First Substitute".)

Red Flag

When displayed by a committee boat, means:
"Leave all *marks* to port."

Green Flag

When displayed by a committee boat, means:
"Leave all *marks* to starboard."

Blue Flag or Shape - Finishing Signal.

When displayed by a committee boat, means:
"The committee boat is on station at the finishing line."

4.2 SPECIAL SIGNALS
The sailing instructions shall designate any other special signals and shall explain their meaning.

4.3   CALLING ATTENTION TO VISUAL SIGNALS

Whenever the race committee makes a signal, except "S" before the warning signal or a blue flag or shape when on station at the finishing line, it shall call attention to its action as follows:

(a)   Three guns or other sound signals when displaying:

     (i)   "N";

     (ii)   "N over X";

     (iii)   "N over First Substitute".

(b)   Two guns or other sound signals when displaying:

     (i)   "AP";

     (ii)   "S";

     (iii)   "First Substitute".

(c)   Repetitive sound signals while displaying Code flag "C".

(d)   One gun or other sound signal when making any other signal, including the lowering of:

     (i)   "AP" when the length of the *postponement* is not signalled;

     (ii)   "N over X";

     (iii)   "First Substitute".

4.4   SIGNALS FOR STARTING A RACE

(a)   Unless otherwise prescribed in the sailing instructions, the signals for starting a race shall be made at five-minute intervals exactly, and shall be either:

System 1	Warning Signal	— Class flag broken out or distinctive signal displayed.
	Preparatory Signal	— Code flag "P" broken out or distinctive signal displayed.
	Starting Signal	— Both warning and preparatory signals lowered.

In System 1, when classes are *started*:

     (i)   at ten-minute intervals—
the warning signal for each succeeding class shall be broken out or displayed at the starting signal of the preceding class.

     (ii)   at five-minute intervals—
the preparatory signal for the first class to *start* shall be left displayed until the last class *starts*. The warning signal for each succeeding class shall be broken out or displayed at the preparatory signal of the preceding class.

or

System 2	Warning Signal	— White or yellow shape or flag.
	Preparatory Signal	— Blue shape or flag.
	Starting Signal	— Red shape or flag.

In System 2, each signal shall be lowered one minute before the next is made.

Class flags when used shall be broken out not later than the preparatory signal for each class.

When classes are *started*:

    (i)   at ten-minute intervals—
           the starting signal for each class shall be the warning signal for the next.

    (ii)   at five-minute intervals—
           the preparatory signal for each class shall be the warning signal for the next.

(b)   Although rules 4.1 "P" and 4.4(a) specify five-minute intervals, the sailing instructions may prescribe any intervals.

(c)   A warning signal shall not be made before its scheduled time, except with the consent of all yachts entitled to *race*.

(d)   When a significant error is made in the timing of the interval between any of the signals for starting a race, the recommended procedure is to signal a general recall, *postponement* or *abandonment* of the race whose start is directly affected by the error and a corresponding *postponement* of succeeding races. Unless otherwise prescribed in the sailing instructions, a new warning signal shall be made. When the race is not recalled, *postponed* or *abandoned* after an error in the timing of the interval, each succeeding signal shall be made at the correct interval from the preceding signal.

4.5   VISUAL STARTING SIGNALS TO GOVERN
        Times shall be taken from the visual starting signals, and a failure or mistiming of a gun or other sound signal calling attention to starting signals shall be disregarded.   **118**

5   Designating the Course, Altering the Course or Race

5.1   Before or with the warning signal for a class that has not *started*, the race committee: **117**

(a)   shall either signal or otherwise designate the course.

(b)   may remove and substitute a new course signal.

5.2   Before the preparatory signal, the race committee may shift a starting *mark*.

5.3   Before the starting signal, the race committee may:

(a)   shorten the course to one prescribed in the sailing instructions.

(b)   *postpone* to designate a new course before or with the new warning signal, or for any other reason.

(c)   *postpone* to a later day.

(d)   *cancel* the race for any reason.

5.4   After the starting signal, the race committee may:

(a)   *abandon* and re-sail the race when there is an error in starting procedure.

(b) when prescribed in the sailing instructions, change the course at any rounding *mark* subject to proper notice being given to each yacht before she begins the changed leg.

(c) shorten the course by finishing a race at any rounding *mark* or as prescribed in the sailing instructions, or *abandon* or *cancel* the race:

   (i) because of foul weather, or

   (ii) because of insufficient wind making it improbable that the race will finish within the time limit, or

   (iii) because a *mark* is missing or has shifted, or

   (iv) for any other reasons directly affecting the safety or fairness of the competition.

5.5 After a race has been completed, the race committee shall not *abandon* or *cancel* it without taking the appropriate action under rule 74.2(b), Consideration of Redress.

5.6 The race committee shall notify all yachts concerned by signal or otherwise when and where a race *postponed* to a later day or *abandoned* will be *sailed*.

6 Starting and Finishing Lines

Unless otherwise prescribed in the sailing instructions, the starting and finishing lines shall be either:

(a) a line between a *mark* and a mast or staff on the committee boat or station clearly identified in the sailing instructions; or

(b) a line between two *marks*; or

(c) the extension of a line through two stationary posts, with or without a *mark* at or near its outer limit, inside which the yachts shall pass.

For types (a) and (c) of starting or finishing lines the sailing instructions may also prescribe that a *mark* will be laid at or near the inner end of the line, in which case yachts shall pass between it and the outer *mark*.

7 Start of a Race

7.1 STARTING AREA
The sailing instructions may define a starting area that may be bounded by buoys; if so, they shall not rank as *marks*.

7.2 TIMING THE START
The *start* of a yacht shall be timed from her starting signal.

8 Recalls

8.1 INDIVIDUAL RECALL
Unless otherwise prescribed in the sailing instructions, when, at her starting signal, any part of a yacht's hull, crew or equipment is on the course side of the starting line or its extensions, or she has not complied with rule 51.1(c), Sailing the Course, the race committee shall promptly display Code flag "X", accompanied by one sound signal, until all such yachts are wholly on the pre-start side of the starting line or its extensions and have complied with rule 51.1(c) when applicable, or for four minutes after the starting signal,

whichever is the earlier. The sailing instructions may prescribe that the race committee will also hail the yacht's sail number.

8.2 GENERAL RECALL

(a) When there is either a number of unidentified premature starters or an error in starting procedure, the race committee may make a general recall signal in accordance with rules 4.1 "First Substitute", Visual Signals, and 4.3, Calling Attention to Visual Signals.

(b) Except as provided in rule 31.2, Rule Infringement, rule infringements before the preparatory signal for the new start shall be disregarded for the purpose of competing in the race to be re-started.

9 Marks

9.1 MARK MISSING

(a) When any *mark* either is missing or has shifted, the race committee shall, when possible, replace it in its stated position, or substitute a new one with similar characteristics or a buoy or vessel displaying Code flag "M" - the *mark* signal.

(b) When it is impossible either to replace the *mark* or to substitute a new one in time for the yachts to round or pass it, the race committee may, at its discretion, act in accordance with rule 5.4(c)(iii), Designating the Course, Altering the Course or Race.

9.2 MARK UNSEEN
When races are *sailed* in fog or at night, dead reckoning alone need not necessarily be accepted as evidence that a *mark* has been rounded or passed.

10 Finishing Within a Time Limit

Unless otherwise prescribed in the sailing instructions, in races where there is a time limit, one yacht *finishing* within the prescribed limit shall make the race valid for all other yachts in that race.

11 Ties

When there is a tie at the finish of a race, either actual or on corrected times, the points for the place for which the yachts have tied and for the place immediately below shall be added together and divided equally. When two or more yachts tie for a trophy or prize in either a single race or a series, the yachts so tied shall, when practicable, *sail* a deciding race; if not, either the tie shall be broken by a method established under rule 3.2(a)(viii), Sailing Instructions, or the yachts so tied shall either receive equal prizes or share the prize.

12 Races to be Re-sailed

When a race is to be re-sailed:

(a) All yachts entered in the original race shall be eligible to *start* in the race to be re-sailed.

(b) Subject to the entry requirements of the original race, and at the discretion of the race committee, new entries may be accepted.

(c) Rule infringements in the original race shall be disregarded for the purpose of competing in the race to be re-sailed.

(d) The race committee shall notify the yachts concerned when and where the race will be re-sailed.

(Numbers 13, 14, 15, 16 and 17 are spare numbers)

Part III—General Requirements

Owner's Responsibilities for Qualifying his Yacht

*A yacht intending to **race** shall, to avoid subsequent disqualification, comply with the rules of Part III before her preparatory signal and, when applicable, while **racing.***

18   Entries

Unless otherwise prescribed either in the notice of race or in the sailing instructions, entries shall be made in the following form:

FORM OF ENTRY

To the Secretary . . . . Club
Please enter the yacht . . . . for
the . . . . race, on the . . . .
her national letters and sail number are . . . .
her rig is . . . .
the colour of her hull is . . . .
and her rating or class is . . . .

I agree to be bound by the racing rules of the IYRU, by the prescriptions of the national authority under which this race is sailed, by the sailing instructions and by the class rules.

> *Name . . . .*
> *Address . . . .*
> *Telephone No. . . . .*
> *Club . . . .*
> *Address during event . . . .*
> *Telephone No. . . . .*

Signed . . . . Date . . . .
  (Owner or owner's representative)
Entrance fee enclosed

19   Measurement or Rating Certificates

19.1   Every yacht entering a race shall hold such valid measurement or rating certificate as is required by the national authority or other duly authorised body, by her class rules, by the notice of race, or by the sailing instructions.

119

19.2   An owner shall be responsible for maintaining his yacht in accordance with her class rules and for ensuring that her certificate is not invalidated by alterations. Deviations in excess of tolerances specified in the class rules caused by normal wear or damage and that do not affect the performance of the yacht shall not invalidate the measurement or rating certificate of the yacht for a particular race, but shall be rectified before she *races* again, unless in the opinion of the race committee there has been no practicable opportunity to rectify the wear or damage.

19.3 (a) The owner of a yacht who cannot produce such a certificate when required, may be permitted to sign and lodge with the race committee, before she *starts*, a statement in the following form:

To the Secretary . . . .*Club*

UNDERTAKING TO PRODUCE CERTIFICATE

The yacht . . . .*competes in the* . . . .
race on condition that a valid certificate previously issued by the authorised administrative body, or a copy of it, is submitted to the race committee before the end of the series, and that she competes in the race(s) on the measurement or rating of that certificate.

　　　　Signed . . . .
　　　　　(Owner or his representative)
　　　　Date . . . .

(b) In this event the sailing instructions may require that the owner shall lodge such a deposit as may be required by the organising authority, which may be forfeited when such certificate or copy is not submitted to the race committee within the prescribed period.

20　Ownership of Yachts

20.1　A yacht shall be eligible to compete only when she is either owned by or on charter to and has been entered by a yacht or sailing club recognised by its national authority or a member or members thereof.

20.2　Two or more yachts owned or chartered wholly or in part by the same body or person shall not compete in the same race without the previous consent of the race committee.

20.3　An owner shall not steer any yacht other than his own in a race wherein his own yacht competes without the previous consent of the race committee.

21　Member on Board

Every yacht shall have on board a member of a yacht or sailing club recognised by its national authority to be in charge of the yacht as owner or owner's representative.

22　Shifting Ballast

22.1　GENERAL RESTRICTIONS
Floorboards shall be kept down; bulkheads and doors left standing; ladders, stairways and water tanks left in place; all cabin, galley and forecastle fixtures and fittings kept on board; all movable ballast shall be properly stowed under the floorboards or in lockers and no dead weight shall be shifted.

22.2　SHIPPING, UNSHIPPING OR SHIFTING BALLAST; WATER
From 2100 on the day before the race until she is no longer *racing*, a yacht shall not ship, unship or shift ballast, whether movable or fixed, or take in or discharge water, except for ordinary ship's use and the removal of bilge water. This rule shall not apply to wearing or carrying clothing, equipment or ballast in compliance with rule 61, Clothing and Equipment.

23 Anchor

Unless otherwise prescribed by her class rules, every yacht shall carry on board an anchor and chain or rope of suitable size.

24 Life-Saving Equipment

Unless otherwise prescribed by her class rules, every yacht shall carry adequate life-saving equipment for all persons on board, one item of which shall be ready for immediate use.

25 Class Insignia, National Letters and Sail Numbers

25.1 Every yacht of an international class recognised by the IYRU shall carry on her mainsail and, as provided in rule 25.3(c), on her spinnaker:

(a) The insignia denoting the class to which she belongs.

(b) A letter or letters showing her nationality, thus:

A	Argentina	H	Holland	PH	Philippines
AE	Dubai	HA	Netherlands	PK	Pakistan
AL	Algeria		Antilles	PR	Puerto Rico
ANU	Antigua	I	Italy	PU	Peru
AR	Egypt	IL	Iceland	PY	Paraguay
B	Belgium	IND	India	PZ	Poland
BA	Bahamas	IR	Ireland	Q	Kuwait
BH	Bahrain	IS	Israel	QA	Qatar
BL	Brazil	J	Japan	RB	Botswana
BR	Burma	K	United	RC	Cuba
BU	Bulgaria		Kingdom	RI	Indonesia
CB	Colombia	KA	Australia	RK	Republic of
CH	China	KB	Bermuda		Korea
CI	Grand Cayman	KBA	Barbados	RM	Roumania
CP	Cyprus	KC	Canada	S	Sweden
CY	Sri Lanka	KF	Fiji	SA	South Africa
CZ	Czechoslovakia	KH	Hong Kong	SE	Senegal
D	Denmark	KJ	Jamaica	SM	San Marino
DDR	German	KK	Kenya	SR	Union of
	Democratic	KP	Papua New		Soviet
	Republic		Guinea		Socialist
DJ	Djibouti	KS	Singapore		Republics
DK	Democratic	KT	Trinidad and	TA	Chinese
	People's		Tobago		Taipei
	Republic of	KV	British Virgin Is.	TH	Thailand
	Korea	KZ	New Zealand	TK	Turkey
DR	Dominican	L	Finland	TN	Tunisia
	Republic	LX	Luxembourg	U	Uruguay
E	Spain	M	Hungary	US	United
EC	Ecuador	MA	Morocco		States of
F	France	MO	Monaco		America
FL	Liechtenstein	MT	Malta	V	Venezuela
G	Federal	MX	Mexico	VI	U.S. Virgin
	Republic of	MY	Malaysia		Is.
	Germany	N	Norway	X	Chile
GM	Guam	OE	Austria	Y	Yugoslavia
GR	Greece	OM	Oman	Z	Switzerland
GU	Guatemala	P	Portugal	ZB	Zimbabwe

National letters need not be carried in home waters, except in an international championship.

(c) (i) A sail number allotted to her by her national authority or, when so prescribed by the class rules, by the international class association.

(ii) When so prescribed by the class rules, an owner may be allotted a personal sail number by the relevant issuing authority, which may be used on all his yachts in that class instead of the sail numbers allotted to such yachts in accordance with rule 25.1(c)(i).

25.2 The following specifications and minimum sizes of national letters and sail numbers shall apply.

(a) They shall be:

(i) clearly visible, legible and, unless otherwise prescribed by the class rules, of a single colour that strongly contrasts with the sail, and

(ii) in roman style (upright), without serifs, with arabic numerals, and with lines that are continuous and of uniform thickness.

(b) The minimum sizes for national letters and sail numbers shall be related to the yacht's overall length (LOA) and shall be as follows:

LOA	Height	Width excl. number 1 and letter I	Thickness	Space between adjoining letters & nos.
Under 3.5 m	230 mm	150 mm	30 mm	45 mm
3.5 m - 8.5 m	300 mm	200 mm	40 mm	60 mm
8.5 m - 11 m	375 mm	250 mm	50 mm	75 mm
Over 11 m	450 mm	300 mm	60 mm	90 mm

The size and style requirements of rules 25.2(a) and (b) shall not apply to sails made prior to 1st May, 1989.

(c) National letters shall be placed in front of or above the sail numbers. When the national letters end in "I" (e.g. Italy, U.S. Virgin Islands) and are placed in front of the numbers, they shall be separated from them by a horizontal line approximately 50 mm long.

25.3 The following positioning of class insignia, national letters and sail numbers on the sail shall apply.

(a) Unless otherwise prescribed by the class rules, the class insignia, national letter(s) and sail numbers shall be above an imaginary line projecting at right angles to the luff from a point one-third of the distance, measured from the tack, to the head of the sail; and shall be placed at different heights on the two sides of the sail, those on the starboard side being uppermost.

(b) Where the class insignia is of such a design that, when placed back to back on the two sides of the sail, they coincide, they may be so placed.

(c) The national letters and sail numbers only shall be similarly placed on both sides of the spinnaker, but at approximately half-height.

25.4 Other yachts shall comply with the rules of their national authority or class |
in regard to the allotment, carrying and size of insignia, letters and numbers,
which rules shall, when practicable, conform to the above requirements.

25.5 When so prescribed in the notice of race or in the sailing instructions, a |
yacht chartered or loaned for an event may carry national letters or sail
numbers in contravention of her class rules. In all other respects the sails
shall comply with the class rules.

25.6 A yacht shall not be disqualified for infringing the provisions of rule 25 |
without prior warning and adequate opportunity to make correction.

26 Event Classification; Advertising

A yacht and her crew shall compete in conformity with Appendix 14, Event
Classification and Advertising.

27 Forestays and Jib Tacks

Unless otherwise prescribed by the class rules, forestays and jib tacks (not
including spinnaker staysails when not *close-hauled*) shall be fixed
approximately in the centre-line of the yacht.

(Numbers 28, 29 and 30 are spare numbers)

Part IV—**Right of Way Rules**

Rights and Obligations when Yachts Meet

*The rules of Part IV do not apply in any way to a vessel that is neither intending to **race** nor **racing**; such vessel shall be treated in accordance with the International Regulations for Preventing Collisions at Sea or Government Right of Way Rules applicable to the area concerned. The rules of Part IV apply only between yachts that are either intending to **race** or are **racing** in the same or different races, and, except when rule 3.2(b)(xxix), Race Continues After Sunset, applies, replace the International Regulations for Preventing Collisions at Sea or Government Right of Way Rules applicable to the area concerned, from the time a yacht intending to **race** begins to **sail** about in the vicinity of the starting line until she has either **finished** or retired and has left the vicinity of the course. (See Appendix 9).*

SECTION A—**Obligations and Penalties**

31 Rule Infringement

31.1 A yacht may be penalised for infringing a rule of Part IV only when the infringement occurs while she is *racing*.

31.2 A yacht may be penalised, before or after she is *racing*, for seriously hindering a yacht that is *racing* or for infringing the sailing instructions.

32 Serious Damage

32.1 AVOIDING COLLISIONS
When a collision has resulted in serious damage, the right-of-way yacht shall be penalised as well as the other yacht when she had the opportunity but failed to make a reasonable attempt to avoid the collision.

32.2 HAILING
Except when *luffing* under rule 38.1, Luffing Rights, a right-of-way yacht that does not hail before or when making an alteration of course that may not be foreseen by the other yacht may be penalised as well as the yacht required to keep clear when a collision resulting in serious damage occurs.

33 Contact between Yachts Racing

When there is contact that is not both minor and unavoidable between the hulls, equipment or crew of two yachts, both shall be penalised unless: either

(a) one of the yachts retires in acknowledgement of the infringement, or exonerates herself by accepting an alternative penalty when so prescribed in the sailing instructions,

or

(b) one or both of these yachts lodges a valid **protest**.

120

120

121

121

34 Maintaining Rights

When a yacht that may have infringed a **rule** does not retire or exonerate herself, other yachts shall continue to accord her such rights as she has under the rules of Part IV.

SECTION B—Principal Right of Way Rules and their Limitations

These rules apply except when over-ridden by a rule in Section C.

35 Limitations on Altering Course

When one yacht is required to keep clear of another, the right-of-way yacht shall not alter course so as to prevent the other yacht from keeping clear, or so as to obstruct her while she is keeping clear, except:

(a)   to the extent permitted by rule 38.1, Luffing Rights, and

(b)   when assuming a *proper course:*
either

  (i)   to *start*, unless subject to rule 40, Same Tack, Luffing before Clearing the Starting Line, or to the second part of rule 44.1(b), Returning to Start,

  or

  (ii)   when rounding a *mark*.

36 Opposite Tacks - Basic Rule

A *port-tack* yacht shall keep clear of a *starboard-tack* yacht.

37 Same Tack - Basic Rules

37.1 WHEN OVERLAPPED
A *windward yacht* shall keep clear of a *leeward yacht*.

37.2 WHEN NOT OVERLAPPED
A yacht *clear astern* shall keep clear of a yacht *clear ahead*.

37.3 TRANSITIONAL
A yacht that establishes an *overlap* to *leeward* from *clear astern* shall initially allow the *windward yacht* ample room and opportunity to keep clear.

38 Same Tack - Luffing after Clearing the Starting Line

38.1 LUFFING RIGHTS
After she has *started* and cleared the starting line, a yacht *clear ahead* or a *leeward yacht* may *luff* as she pleases, subject to the following limitations of this rule.

38.2 LIMITATIONS

  (a)   Proper Course Limitations:
A *leeward yacht* shall not *sail* above her *proper course* while an *overlap* exists, if when the *overlap* began or at any time during its existence,

the helmsman of the *windward yacht* (when sighting abeam from his normal station and *sailing* no higher than the *leeward yacht*) has been abreast or forward of the mainmast of the *leeward yacht*.

(b) Overlap Limitations:

For the purpose of rule 38 only: An *overlap* does not exist unless the yachts are clearly within two overall lengths of the longer yacht; and an *overlap* that exists between two yachts when the leading yacht *starts*, or when one or both of them completes a *tack* or *gybe*, shall be regarded as a new *overlap* beginning at that time.

(c) Hailing to Stop or Prevent a Luff:

When there is doubt, the *leeward yacht* may assume that she has the right to *luff* or *sail* above her *proper course* unless the helmsman of the *windward yacht* has hailed either:

(i) "Mast Abeam", or words to that effect, or

(ii) "Obstruction", or words to that effect.

The *leeward yacht* shall be governed by such hail and curtail her *luff*. When she deems the hail improper, her only remedy is to protest.

(d) Curtailing a Luff:

The *windward yacht* shall not cause a *luff* to be curtailed because of her proximity to the *leeward yacht* unless an *obstruction*, a third yacht or other object restricts her ability to respond.

(e) Luffing Rights over Two or More Yachts:

A yacht shall not *luff* unless she has the right to *luff* all yachts that would be affected by her *luff*, in which case they shall all respond, even when an intervening yacht or yachts would not otherwise have the right to *luff*.

39 Same Tack - Sailing below a Proper Course after Starting

A yacht that is on a free leg of the course shall not *sail* below her *proper course* when she is clearly within three of her overall lengths of a *leeward yacht* or of a yacht *clear astern* that is steering a course to *leeward* of her own.

40 Same Tack - Luffing before Clearing the Starting Line

Before a yacht *clear ahead* or a *leeward yacht* has *started* and cleared the starting line, any *luff* on her part that causes another yacht to have to alter course to avoid a collision shall be carried out slowly and initially in such a way as to give a *windward yacht* room and opportunity to keep clear. Furthermore, the *leeward yacht* shall not so *luff* above a *close-hauled* course while the helmsman of the *windward yacht* (sighting abeam from his normal station) is abreast or forward of the mainmast of the *leeward yacht*. Rules 38.2(c), Hailing to Stop or Prevent a Luff; 38.2(d), Curtailing a Luff; and 38.2(e), Luffing Rights over Two or More Yachts, also apply.

41 Changing Tacks - Tacking and Gybing

41.1 BASIC RULE

A yacht that is either *tacking* or *gybing* shall keep clear of a yacht *on a tack*.

41.2 TRANSITIONAL

A yacht shall neither *tack* nor *gybe* into a position that will give her right of way unless she does so far enough from a yacht *on a tack* to enable this yacht to keep clear without having to begin to alter her course until after the *tack* or *gybe* has been completed.

41.3 ONUS
A yacht that *tacks* or *gybes* has the onus of satisfying the **protest committee** that she completed her *tack* or *gybe* in accordance with rule 41.2.

41.4 WHEN SIMULTANEOUS
When two yachts are both *tacking* or both *gybing* at the same time, the one on the other's port side shall keep clear.

SECTION C—Rules that Apply at Marks and Obstructions and other Exceptions to the Rules of Section B

When a rule of this section applies, to the extent to which it explicitly provides rights and obligations, it over-rides any conflicting rule of Section B, Principal Right of Way Rules and their Limitations, except rule 35, Limitations on Altering Course.

42 Rounding or Passing Marks and Obstructions

Rule 42 applies when yachts are about to round or pass a *mark* on the same required side or an *obstruction* on the same side, except that it shall not apply:

(a) between two yachts on opposite *tacks:*

    (i)   when they are on a beat, or

    (ii)   when one, but not both, of them will have to *tack* either to round or pass the *mark* or to avoid the *obstruction*, or

(b) when rule 42.4 applies.

42.1 WHEN OVERLAPPED

An Outside Yacht

(a) An outside yacht shall give each inside *overlapping* yacht room to round or pass the *mark* or *obstruction*, except as provided in rule 42.3. Room is the space needed by an inside *overlapping* yacht that is handled in a seamanlike manner in the prevailing conditions to pass in safety between an outside yacht and a *mark* or *obstruction*, and includes space to *tack* or *gybe* when either is an integral part of the rounding or passing manoeuvre.

(b) An outside yacht *overlapped* when she comes within two of her overall lengths of a *mark* or *obstruction* shall give room as required, even though the *overlap* may thereafter be broken.

(c) An outside yacht that claims to have broken an *overlap* has the onus of satisfying the **protest committee** that she became *clear ahead* when she was more than two of her overall lengths from the *mark* or *obstruction*.

An Inside Yacht

(d) A yacht that claims an inside *overlap* has the onus of satisfying the **protest committee** that she established the *overlap* in accordance with rule 42.3.

(e) When an inside yacht of two or more *overlapped* yachts, either on opposite *tacks* or on the same *tack* without *luffing* rights, will have to *gybe* in order most directly to assume a *proper course* to the next *mark*, she shall *gybe* at the first reasonable opportunity.

Hailing

(f) A yacht that hails when claiming the establishment or termination of an *overlap* or insufficiency of room at a *mark* or *obstruction* thereby helps to support her claim.

42.2 WHEN NOT OVERLAPPED

A Yacht Clear Astern

(a) A yacht *clear astern* when the yacht *clear ahead* comes within two of her overall lengths of a *mark* or *obstruction* shall keep clear in anticipation of and during the rounding or passing manoeuvre, whether the yacht *clear ahead* remains on the same *tack* or *gybes*.

(b) A yacht *clear astern* shall not *luff* above *close-hauled* so as to prevent a yacht *clear ahead* from *tacking* to round a *mark*.

A Yacht Clear Ahead

(c) A yacht *clear ahead* that *tacks* to round a *mark* is subject to rule 41, Changing Tacks - Tacking and Gybing.

(d) A yacht *clear ahead* shall be under no obligation to give room to a yacht *clear astern* before an *overlap* is established.

42.3 LIMITATIONS

(a) Limitation on Establishing an Overlap
A yacht that establishes an inside *overlap* from *clear astern* is entitled to room under rule 42.1(a) only when, at that time, the outside yacht:

(i) is able to give room, and

(ii) is more than two of her overall lengths from the *mark* or *obstruction*. However, when a yacht completes a *tack* within two of her overall lengths of a *mark* or *obstruction*, she shall give room as required by rule 42.1(a) to a yacht that, by *luffing*, cannot thereafter avoid establishing a late inside *overlap*.

At a continuing *obstruction*, rule 42.3(b) applies.

(b) Limitation When an Obstruction is a Continuing One.
A yacht *clear astern* may establish an *overlap* between a yacht *clear ahead* and a continuing *obstruction*, such as a shoal or the shore or another vessel, only when, at that time, there is room for her to pass between them in safety.

42.4 AT A STARTING MARK SURROUNDED BY NAVIGABLE WATER
When approaching the starting line to *start* until clearing the starting *marks* after *starting*, a *leeward yacht* shall be under no obligation to give any *windward yacht* room to pass to leeward of a starting *mark* surrounded

by navigable water, including such a *mark* that is also an *obstruction*; but, after the starting signal, a *leeward yacht* shall not deprive a *windward yacht* of room at such a *mark* by *sailing* either:

(a) to windward of the compass bearing of the course to the next *mark*, or

(b) above *close-hauled*.

43 Close-Hauled, Hailing for Room to Tack at Obstructions

43.1 HAILING

When two *close-hauled* yachts are on the same *tack* and safe pilotage requires the yacht *clear ahead* or the *leeward yacht* to make a substantial alteration of course to clear an *obstruction*, and when she intends to *tack*, but cannot *tack* without colliding with the other yacht, she shall hail the other yacht for room to *tack* and clear the other yacht, but she shall not hail and *tack* simultaneously.

153
154
155

43.2 RESPONDING

The hailed yacht at the earliest possible moment after the hail shall either:

(a) *tack*, in which case the hailing yacht shall begin to *tack* immediately she is able to *tack* and clear the other yacht; or

(b) reply "You *tack*", or words to that effect, in which case:

   (i) the hailing yacht shall immediately *tack* and

   (ii) the hailed yacht shall give the hailing yacht room to *tack* and clear her.

   (iii) The onus of satisfying the **protest committee** that she gave sufficient room shall lie on the hailed yacht that replied "You *tack*".

43.3 WHEN AN OBSTRUCTION IS ALSO A MARK

(a) When an *obstruction* is a starting *mark* surrounded by navigable water, or the ground tackle of such a *mark*, and when approaching the starting line to *start* and after *starting*, the yacht *clear ahead* or the *leeward yacht* shall not be entitled to room to *tack*.

155
156

(b) At other *obstructions* that are *marks*, when the hailed yacht can fetch the *obstruction*, the hailing yacht shall not be entitled to room to *tack* and clear the hailed yacht, and the hailed yacht shall immediately so inform the hailing yacht. When, thereafter, the hailing yacht again hails for room to *tack* and clear the hailed yacht, the hailed yacht shall, at the earliest possible moment after the hail, give the hailing yacht the required room. After receiving room, the hailing yacht shall either retire immediately or exonerate herself by accepting an alternative penalty when so prescribed in the sailing instructions.

156
157

(c) When, after having refused to respond to a hail under rule 43.3(b), the hailed yacht fails to fetch, she shall retire immediately or exonerate herself by accepting an alternative penalty when so prescribed in the sailing instructions.

157

44 Returning to Start

44.1 (a) After the starting signal, a premature starter returning to *start*, or a yacht working into position from the course side of the starting line or its extensions, shall keep clear of all yachts that are *starting* or have *started* correctly, until she is wholly on the pre-start side of the starting line or its extensions.

(b)   Thereafter, she shall be accorded the rights under the rules of Part IV of a yacht that is *starting* correctly; but when she thereby acquires right of way over another yacht that is *starting* correctly, she shall allow that yacht ample room and opportunity to keep clear.

44.2   A premature starter, while continuing to *sail* the course and until it is obvious that she is returning to *start*, shall be accorded the rights under the rules of Part IV of a yacht that has *started*.

45   Keeping Clear after Touching a Mark

45.1   A yacht that has touched a *mark* and is exonerating herself shall keep clear of all other yachts until she has completed her exoneration and, when she has *started*, is on a *proper course* to the next *mark*.

45.2   A yacht that has touched a *mark*, while continuing to *sail* the course and until it is obvious that she is exonerating herself, shall be accorded rights under the rules of Part IV.

46   Person Overboard; Yacht Anchored, Aground or Capsized

46.1   A yacht under way shall keep clear of another yacht *racing* that:

(a)   is manoeuvring or hailing for the purpose of rescuing a person overboard, or

(b)   is anchored, aground or capsized.

46.2   A yacht shall not be penalised when she is unable to avoid fouling a yacht that she is attempting to assist or that goes aground or is capsized.

46.3   A yacht is capsized from the time her masthead is in the water until her masthead is clear of the water and she has steerage way.

46.4   A yacht anchored or aground shall indicate the fact to any yacht that may be in danger of fouling her. Under normal conditions, a hail is sufficient indication. Of two yachts anchored, the one that anchored later shall keep clear, except that a yacht dragging shall keep clear of one that is not.

(Numbers 47, 48 and 49 are spare numbers)

Part V—Other Sailing Rules

Obligations in Handling a Yacht

*A yacht is subject to the rules of Part V only while she is **racing**.*

50   Ranking as a Starter

A yacht whose entry has been accepted and that *sails* about in the vicinity of the starting line between her preparatory and starting signals shall rank as a starter whether she *starts* or not.

162

51   Sailing the Course

51.1   (a)   A yacht shall *start* and *finish* only as prescribed in the starting and finishing definitions.

162

(b)   When any part of a yacht's hull, crew or equipment is on the course side of the starting line or its extensions at the starting signal, she shall thereafter *start* in accordance with the definition.

(c)   When Code flag "I" has been displayed, and when any part of a yacht's hull, crew or equipment is on the course side of the starting line or its extensions during the minute before her starting signal, she shall *sail* to the pre-start side of the line across one of its extensions and *start*.

(d)   Failure of a yacht to see or hear her recall signal shall not relieve her of her obligation to *start* correctly.

51.2   A yacht shall *sail* the course so as to round or pass each *mark* on the required side in correct sequence, and so that a string representing her wake, from the time she *starts* until she *finishes*, would, when drawn taut, lie on the required side of each *mark*, touching each rounding *mark*.

163

51.3   A *mark* has a required side for a yacht as long as she is on a leg that it begins, bounds or ends. A starting line *mark* begins to have a required side for a yacht when she *starts*. A starting limit *mark* has a required side for a yacht from the time she is approaching the starting line to *start* until she has left the *mark* astern on the first leg. A finishing line *mark* and a finishing limit *mark* cease to have a required side for a yacht when she *finishes*.

163
164

51.4   A yacht that rounds or passes a *mark* on the wrong side may exonerate herself by making her course conform to the requirements of rule 51.2.

163

51.5   It is not necessary for a yacht to cross the finishing line completely; after *finishing*, she may clear it in either direction.

164

52   Touching a Mark

52.1   A yacht shall neither:

(a)   touch:

(i)   a starting *mark* before *starting*, or

(ii)   a *mark* that begins, bounds or ends the leg of the course on which she is *sailing*, or

165
166

(iii)   a finishing *mark* after *finishing* and before clearing the finishing line and *marks*,

nor

(b)   cause a *mark* or *mark* vessel to shift to avoid being touched.

52.2   (a)   When a yacht infringes rule 52.1, she may exonerate herself by *sailing* well clear of all other yachts as soon as possible after the incident, and remaining clear while she makes two complete 360° turns (720°) in the same direction, including two *tacks* and two *gybes*.

(b)   When a yacht touches a finishing *mark,* she shall not rank as having *finished* until she first completes her turns and thereafter *finishes*.

52.3   When a yacht is wrongfully compelled by another yacht to infringe rule 52.1, she shall be exonerated:

(a)   by the retirement of the other yacht (or by the other yacht accepting an alternative penalty when so prescribed in the sailing instructions) in acknowledgement of the infringement, or

(b)   in accordance with rule 74.4(b), Penalties and Exoneration, after lodging a valid **protest**.

53   Casting Off, Anchoring, Making Fast and Hauling Out

53.1   AT THE PREPARATORY SIGNAL
A yacht shall be afloat and off moorings at her preparatory signal, but may be anchored.

53.2   WHEN RACING
A yacht may anchor, but shall not make fast or be made fast by means other than anchoring, nor be hauled out, except for the purpose of rule 55, Aground or Foul of an Obstruction, or to effect repairs, reef sails or bail out.

53.3   MEANS OF ANCHORING
Means of anchoring may include the crew standing on the bottom or any weight lowered to the bottom. A yacht shall recover any anchor or weight used, and any chain or rope attached to it, before continuing in the race, unless, after making every effort, she fails to do so. In this case she shall report the circumstances to the race committee, which may penalise her when it considers the loss due either to inadequate gear or to insufficient effort to recover it.

54   Propulsion

54.1   BASIC RULE
Except when permitted by rule 54.3, a yacht shall compete only by *sailing*, and her crew shall not otherwise move their bodies to propel the yacht. Fundamental Rule A, Rendering Assistance, and rule 55, Aground or Foul of an Obstruction, over-ride rule 54.

54.2   PROHIBITED ACTIONS
Without limiting the application of rule 54.1, these actions are prohibited:

(a)   pumping—repeated fanning of any sail either by trimming and releasing the sail or by vertical or athwartships body movement;

(b) rocking—repeated rolling of the yacht induced either by body movement or adjustment of the sails or centreboard;

(c) ooching—sudden forward body movement, stopped abruptly;

(d) sculling—repeated movement of the helm not necessary for steering;

(e) repeated *tacks* or *gybes* unrelated to changes in the wind or to tactical considerations.

54.3 EXCEPTIONS

(a) Immediately before, during and immediately after a *tack* or *gybe*, the yacht's crew may move their bodies to roll the yacht, provided that such movements do not:

   (i) advance the yacht further in the race than she would have advanced in the absence of the *tack* or *gybe*, or

   (ii) move her mast away from the vertical more than once.

(b) On a free leg of the course, when surfing (rapidly accelerating down the leeward side of a wave) or planing is possible, the yacht's crew may, in order to initiate surfing or planing, pump the sheet, but not the guy, controlling any sail, but only once for each wave or gust of wind. When the mainsail is pumped, only that part of the sheet between the crew member handling the sheet and the first block on the boom shall be used.

(c) Class rules may alter or add to rule 54.3(b).

55 Aground or Foul of an Obstruction

A yacht, after grounding or fouling another vessel or other object, is subject to rule 57, Manual and Stored Power, and may, in getting clear, use her own anchors, boats, ropes, spars and other gear; may send out an anchor in a boat; may be refloated by her crew going overboard either to stand on the bottom or to go ashore to push off; but may receive outside assistance only from the crew of the vessel fouled. A yacht shall recover all her own gear used in getting clear before continuing in the race.

56 Sounding

Any means of sounding may be used, provided that rule 54, Propulsion, is not infringed.

57 Manual and Stored Power

A yacht's standing rigging, running rigging, spars and movable hull appendages shall be adjusted and operated by manual power only, and no device shall be used for these operations that derives assistance from stored energy for doing work. A power winch or windlass may be used in weighing anchor or in getting clear after running aground or fouling any object, and a power pump may be used in an auxiliary yacht.

58 Boarding

Unless otherwise prescribed in the sailing instructions, no person shall board a yacht, except for the purposes of Fundamental Rule A, Rendering Assistance, or to attend an injured or ill member of the crew or temporarily as one of the crew of a vessel fouled.

59 Leaving, Crew Overboard

Unless otherwise prescribed in the sailing instructions, no person on board a yacht when she begins *racing* shall leave, unless injured or ill, or for the purposes of Fundamental Rule A, Rendering Assistance, except that any member of the crew may fall overboard or leave her to swim, stand on the bottom as a means of anchoring, haul her out ashore to effect repairs, reef sails or bail out, or to help her to get clear after grounding or fouling another vessel or object, provided that this person is back on board before the yacht continues in the race.

60 Outside Assistance

Except as permitted by Fundamental Rule A, Rendering Assistance, rule 55, Aground or Foul of an Obstruction, and rule 58, Boarding, a yacht shall neither receive outside assistance nor use any gear other than that on board when her preparatory signal was made.

61 Clothing and Equipment

61.1 (a) Except as permitted by rule 61.2, a competitor shall not wear or carry clothing or equipment for the purpose of increasing his weight.

(b) Furthermore, the total weight of clothing and equipment worn or carried by a competitor shall not be capable of exceeding 15 kilograms, when soaked with water and weighed as provided in Appendix 10, Weighing of Wet Clothing, unless class rules or the sailing instructions prescribe a lesser or greater weight, in which case such weight shall apply, except that it shall not exceed 20 kilograms.

61.2 When so prescribed by the class rules, weight jackets of non-metallic material (excepting normal fasteners), with or without pockets, compartments or containers, shall be permitted, provided that the jacket:

(a) is permanently buoyant,

(b) does not extend more than 30 mm above the competitor's shoulders, and

(c) can be removed by the competitor in less than ten seconds,

and that ballast carried in the pockets, compartments and containers shall only be water. For the purpose of rule 61.1(b), the pockets, compartments and containers shall be filled completely with water and included in the total weight.

61.3 When a competitor is protested or selected for inspection, he shall produce all containers referred to in rule 61.2 that were carried while *racing*.

61.4 Unless otherwise prescribed in the sailing instructions, rule 61.1(b) shall not apply in events for cruiser-racer type yachts required to be equipped with lifelines.

62 Increasing Stability

(a) Unless otherwise prescribed by the class rules, a yacht shall not use any device, such as a trapeze or plank, to project outboard the weight of any of the crew.

(b) When lifelines are required by the class rules or the sailing instructions, no crew member shall station any part of his torso outside them, except when it is necessary to perform a task, and then only temporarily. On yachts equipped with upper and lower lifelines of wire, a crew member sitting on the deck facing outboard with his waist inside the lower lifeline may have the upper part of his body outside the upper lifeline.

63 Skin Friction

A yacht:

(a) shall not eject or release from a container any substance (such as polymer), or

(b) unless otherwise prescribed by her class rules, shall not have specially textured hull or appendage surfaces,

the purpose of which is, or could be, to reduce the frictional resistance of her surface by altering the character of the flow of water inside the boundary layer.

64 Setting and Sheeting Sails

64.1 CHANGING SAILS
While changing headsails and spinnakers, a replacing sail may be fully set and trimmed before the sail it replaces is taken in, but only one mainsail and, except when changing, only one spinnaker shall be carried set.

64.2 SPINNAKER BOOMS
Only one spinnaker boom shall be used at a time and, when in use, shall be attached to and carried only on the side of the foremost mast opposite to the main boom and shall be fixed to the mast.

64.3 SPINNAKERS
A spinnaker, including a headsail set as a spinnaker, shall not be set without a boom. The tack of a spinnaker that is set and drawing shall be in close proximity to the outboard end of the spinnaker boom, except when hoisting, gybing or lowering the spinnaker.

64.4 USE OF OUTRIGGERS

(a) No sail shall be sheeted over or through an outrigger, except as permitted in rule 64.4(b). An outrigger is any fitting or other device so placed that it could exert outward pressure on a sheet or sail at a point from which, with the yacht upright, a vertical line would fall outside the hull or deck planking. For the purpose of this rule: bulwarks, rails and rubbing strakes are not part of the hull or deck planking. A boom of a boomed headsail that requires no adjustment when *tacking* is not an outrigger.

(b) (i) Any sail may be sheeted to or led above a boom regularly used for a working sail and permanently attached to the mast from which the head of the working sail is set.

(ii) A headsail may be sheeted or attached at its clew to a spinnaker boom, provided that a spinnaker is not set.

64.5 HEADSAILS
The following distinction shall apply between spinnakers and headsails. A

169

headsail is a sail in which the mid-girth, measured from the mid-points of the luff and leech, does not exceed 50% of the length of the foot, and in which any other intermediate girth does not exceed a value similarly proportional to its distance from the head of the sail. A sail tacked down abaft the foremost mast is not a headsail.

64.6 CLASS RULES
Class rules may alter or add to this rule.

65 Flags

A national authority may prescribe the flag usage that shall be observed by yachts under its jurisdiction.

66 Fog Signals and Lights

Every yacht shall observe the International Regulations for Preventing Collisions at Sea or Government Rules for fog signals and, as a minimum, the exhibition of lights at night.

(Number 67 is a spare number)

Part VI—**Protests, Penalties and Appeals**

Definitions

*When a term defined below is used in its defined sense, it is printed in **bold** type. The definitions rank as rules.*

Rules -

(a)   These racing rules,

(b)   the prescriptions of the national authority concerned, when they apply,

(c)   the sailing instructions,

(d)   the appropriate class rules, and

(e)   any other conditions governing the event.

Protest - An allegation by a yacht under rule 68, Protests by Yachts, that another yacht has infringed a **rule** or **rules.**

The term **protest** includes when appropriate:

(a)   a request for redress under rule 69, Requests for Redress; or

(b)   a request for a hearing under rule 70.1(c), Action by Race or Protest Committee, or Appendix 3, paragraph 2.6, Alternative Penalties; or

(c)   a notification of a hearing under rule 70.2, Action by Race or Protest Committee; or

(d)   an investigation of redress under rule 70.3, Yacht Materially Prejudiced; or

(e)   a report by a measurer under rule 70.4, Measurer's Responsibility.

Parties to a Protest - The protesting yacht, the protested yacht and any other yacht involved in the incident that might be penalised as a result of the **protest;** and the race committee when it is involved in a **protest** pertaining to rule 69(a), Requests for Redress, or rule 70, Action by Race or Protest Committee.

Protest Committee - The body appointed to hear and decide **protests** in accordance with rule 1.4, Protest Committees, namely:

(a)   the race committee or a sub-committee thereof; or

(b)   a separate and independent protest committee or jury; or

(c)   an international jury.

Interested Party - Anyone who stands to gain or lose as a result of a decision of a **protest committee** or who has a close personal interest in the result.

SECTION A—Initiation of Action

68   Protests by Yachts

68.1 RIGHT TO PROTEST
A yacht can protest any other yacht, except that a **protest** for an alleged infringement of the rules of Part IV can be made only by a yacht directly involved in or witnessing an incident.

68.2 INFORMING THE PROTESTED YACHT
A protesting yacht shall try to inform the yacht she intends to protest that a **protest** will be lodged. When an alternative penalty is prescribed in the sailing instructions, she shall hail the other yacht immediately.

68.3 DURING A RACE - PROTEST FLAG

(a)   An intention to protest an infringement of the **rules** occurring during a race shall be signified by the protesting yacht conspicuously displaying a flag. Code flag "B" is always acceptable, irrespective of any other provisions in the sailing instructions.

(b)   The flag shall be displayed at the first reasonable opportunity after the incident.

(c)   (i)   Except as provided in rule 68.3(c)(ii), the flag shall be displayed until the yacht *finishes* or, when the first opportunity occurs after *finishing*, until acknowledged by the race committee.

    (ii)   In the case of a yacht *sailed* single-handed, it will be sufficient to display the flag at the first reasonable opportunity after the incident and to have it acknowledged by the race committee when the protesting yacht *finishes*.

(d)   When the yacht retires, the flag shall be displayed until she has informed the race committee or has left the vicinity of the course.

68.4 EXCEPTION TO PROTEST FLAG REQUIREMENT
A yacht may protest without having displayed a protest flag when either:

(a)   she has no knowledge of the facts justifying a **protest** until she has *finished* or retired, or

(b)   having been a witness not directly involved in the incident, she learns that a yacht that displayed a protest flag has failed to lodge a valid **protest** in accordance with rule 33(b), Contact between Yachts Racing, or rule 52.3(b), Touching a Mark.

68.5 PARTICULARS TO BE INCLUDED
A **protest** shall be in writing and be signed by the owner or his representative, and include the following particulars.

(a)   the identity of the yacht being protested;

(b)   the date, time and whereabouts of the incident;

(c)   the particular **rule** or **rules** alleged to have been infringed;

(d)   a description of the incident;

(e)   unless irrelevant, a diagram of the incident.

68.6 TIME LIMIT

A protesting yacht shall lodge her **protest** with the race committee:

(a) within two hours of the time she *finishes* the race or within such time as may have been prescribed in the sailing instructions, unless the **protest committee** has reason to extend this time limit, or

(b) when she does not *finish* the race, within such time as the **protest committee** considers reasonable in the circumstances.

68.7 FEE
Unless otherwise prescribed in the sailing instructions, a **protest** shall not be accompanied by a fee.

68.8 REMEDYING DEFECTS IN THE PROTEST
The **protest committee** shall allow the protesting yacht to remedy during the hearing:

(a) any defect in the particulars required by rule 68.5, provided that the **protest** identifies the nature of the incident, and

(b) a failure to deposit such fee as may be required under rule 68.7.

68.9 WITHDRAWING A PROTEST
When a written **protest** has been lodged, it shall not be withdrawn, but shall be decided by the **protest committee,** unless prior to the hearing one or more of the yachts acknowledges the infringement, except that, when the **protest committee** finds that contact between two yachts was minor and unavoidable, a protesting yacht may withdraw her **protest.**

69 **Requests for Redress**

A yacht that alleges that her finishing position has been materially prejudiced through no fault of her own by:

(a) an action or omission of the race committee or **protest committee,** or

(b) rendering assistance in accordance with Fundamental Rule A, Rendering Assistance, or

(c) being damaged by another vessel that was required to keep clear, or

(d) a yacht infringing Fundamental Rule C, Fair Sailing, or against which a penalty has been imposed under rule 75.1, Penalties by the Race Committee or Protest Committee,

may request redress from the **protest committee** in accordance with the requirements for a **protest** provided in rules 68.5, 68.6, 68.7 and 68.8, Protests by Yachts. A protest flag need not be displayed. The **protest committee** shall then proceed in accordance with rule 74.2, Consideration of Redress.

70 **Action by Race or Protest Committee**

70.1 WITHOUT A HEARING

(a) The race committee may act in accordance with rule 74.4, Penalties and Exoneration, without a hearing against a yacht that fails either to *start* or *finish.*

(b) The **protest committee** may act as provided in rule 70.1(a) against

169

a yacht that infringes rule 54.2 or 54.3, Propulsion.

(c) A yacht so penalised shall be entitled to a hearing upon request, and shall be informed of the action taken, either by letter or notification in the race results, or by such other means as the sailing instructions may prescribe.

70.2 WITH A HEARING
The race committee or the **protest committee** may call a hearing when it:

(a) sees an apparent infringement by a yacht of any of the **rules** (except as provided in rule 70.1), or

(b) learns directly from a written or oral statement by a yacht (including one contained in an invalid **protest**) that she may have infringed a **rule,** or

(c) has reasonable grounds for believing that an infringement resulted in serious damage, or

(d) receives a report not later than the same day from a witness who was neither competing in the race nor otherwise an **interested party,** alleging an infringement, or

(e) has reasonable grounds for supposing, from the evidence at the hearing of a valid **protest,** that any yacht involved in the incident may have committed an infringement.

For such hearings, the race committee or **protest committee** shall notify each yacht involved thereof in writing, delivered or mailed not later than 1800 on the day after:

    (i)   the finish of the race, or

    (ii)   the receipt of the relevant information, or

    (iii)   the hearing of the **protest.**

When rule 70.2(e) applies, or rule 70.2(b) after a **protest** has been declared invalid at a hearing, this notice may be given orally at the hearing. The notice shall identify the incident, the **rule** or **rules** alleged to have been infringed and the time and place of the hearing.

70.3 YACHT MATERIALLY PREJUDICED
The race committee or the **protest committee** may initiate consideration of redress when it is satisfied that any of the circumstances set out in rule 69, Requests for Redress, may have occurred.

70.4 MEASURER'S RESPONSIBILITY
When a measurer concludes that a yacht does not comply with her class rules or measurement or rating certificate:

(a) before a race: he shall request the owner or his representative to correct the defect. When the defect is not corrected, he shall report the matter in writing to the race committee, which shall reject or rescind the yacht's entry or approve the entry in accordance with rule 19, Measurement or Rating Certificates. The yacht shall be entitled to a hearing upon request.

(b) after a race: he shall make a report to the race committee or to the **protest committee,** which shall then notify the yacht concerned and call a hearing.

169

The measurer shall not have the authority either to rescind an entry or to disqualify a yacht.

SECTION B—Protest Procedure

71 Procedural Requirements

71.1 REQUIREMENT FOR A HEARING

A yacht shall not be penalised without a hearing, except as provided in rule 70.1, Action by Race or Protest Committee.

71.2 INTERESTED PARTIES

(a) No member of a **protest committee** shall take part in the discussion or decision upon any disputed question in which he is an **interested party,** but this does not preclude him from giving evidence in such a case.

(b) A **party to a protest** who wishes to object to a member of the **protest committee** on the grounds that he is an **interested party** shall do so before evidence is taken at the hearing or as soon thereafter as he becomes aware of the conflict of interest.

71.3 PROTESTS BETWEEN YACHTS IN SEPARATE RACES

A **protest** occurring between yachts competing in separate races organised by different clubs shall be heard by a combined committee of the clubs concerned.

72 Notification of Parties

The **parties to the protest** shall be notified of the time and place of the hearing, and the **protest**, or copies of it, shall be made available to them. A reasonable time shall be allowed for the preparation of a defence.

73 Hearings

73.1 RIGHT TO BE PRESENT

The **parties to the protest,** or a representative of each, shall have the right to be present throughout the hearing of all the evidence and to question witnesses. When there is an alleged infringement of a rule of Parts IV or V, the representatives of yachts shall have been on board at the time of the incident, unless the **protest committee** has reasonable grounds for ruling otherwise. Each witness, unless he is a member of the **protest committee,** shall be excluded, except when giving his evidence. Others may be admitted as observers at the discretion of the **protest committee.**

73.2 ACCEPTANCE OR REFUSAL OF A PROTEST

When the **protest committee** decides that the requirements of rule 68, Protests by Yachts, and of the sailing instructions have been met, the **protest** is valid, and the **protest committee** shall proceed with the hearing. When these requirements are not met, the **protest** is invalid and shall be refused, but such a decision shall not be reached without giving the protesting party an opportunity of bringing evidence that all requirements have been met.

73.3 TAKING OF EVIDENCE
The **protest committee** shall take the evidence presented by the **parties to the protest** and such other evidence as it deems necessary.

73.4 EVIDENCE OF COMMITTEE MEMBER
Any member of the **protest committee** who speaks of his own observation of the incident shall give his evidence as a witness in the presence of the **parties to the protest,** and may be questioned.

73.5 FAILURE TO ATTEND
Failure on the part of any **party to the protest,** or a representative, to make an effort to attend the hearing may justify the **protest committee** in deciding the **protest** as it thinks fit without a full hearing.

73.6 RE-OPENING A HEARING

(a) A hearing may be re-opened when the **protest committee** decides that it may have made a significant error or when material new evidence becomes available within a reasonable time. A **party to the protest** may request such a re-opening, provided that the request is lodged before 1800 on the day following the decision, unless the **protest committee** has reason to extend this time limit.

(b) When the hearing of a **protest** is re-opened, a majority of the members of the **protest committee** shall, when possible, be members of the original **protest committee.**

74   Decisions and Penalties

74.1 FINDING OF FACTS
The **protest committee** shall determine the facts and base its decision upon them. The finding of facts shall not be subject to appeal.

74.2 CONSIDERATION OF REDRESS

(a) When consideration of redress has been initiated as provided in rule 69, Requests for Redress, or rule 70.3, Yacht Materially Prejudiced, the **protest committee** shall decide whether the finishing position of a yacht or yachts has been materially prejudiced in any of the circumstances set out in rule 69.

(b) If so, the **protest committee** shall satisfy itself by taking appropriate evidence, especially before *abandoning* or *cancelling* the race, that it is aware of the relevant facts and of the probable consequences of any arrangement, to all yachts concerned for that particular race and for the series, if any, as a whole.

(c) The **protest committee** shall then make as equitable arrangement as possible for all yachts concerned. This may be to let the results of the race stand, to adjust the points score or the finishing time of the prejudiced yacht, to *abandon* or *cancel* the race or to adopt some other means.

74.3 MEASUREMENT PROTESTS

(a) A **protest** under rule 19, Measurement or Rating Certificates, or class rules that a measurement, scantling or flotation rule has been infringed while *racing,* or that a classification or rating certificate is invalid, may be decided by the **protest committee** immediately after the hearing, provided that it is satisfied there is no reasonable doubt as to the interpretation or application of the rules. When the **protest committee** is not so satisfied, it shall refer the question, together with the facts found, to an authority qualified to resolve such questions. The **protest committee,** in making its decision, shall be governed by the report of the authority.

(b) In addition to the requirements of rule 74.6, the body that issued the certificate of the yacht concerned shall also be notified.

(c) When an appeal under rule 77, Right of Appeal and Decisions, is lodged, the yacht may compete in further races, but subject to the results of that appeal.

74.4 PENALTIES AND EXONERATION
When the **protest committee** after finding the facts, or the race committee or **protest committee** acting under rule 70.1, Action by Race or Protest Committee, decides that:

(a) a yacht has infringed any of the **rules,** or

(b) in consequence of her neglect of any of the **rules,** a yacht has compelled other yachts to infringe any of the **rules,**

she shall be disqualified, unless the sailing instructions applicable to that race provide some other penalty, and, in the case of (b), the other yachts shall be exonerated. Such disqualification or other penalty shall be imposed irrespective of whether the **rule** that led to the disqualification or penalty was mentioned in the **protest,** or the yacht that was at fault was mentioned or protested, e.g., the protesting yacht or a third yacht may be disqualified and the protested yacht exonerated.

74.5 POINTS AND PLACES

(a) When a yacht either is disqualified or has retired after *finishing,* the following yachts shall each be moved up one place.

(b) When a yacht is penalised by being removed from a series or a part of a series, no races are to be re-scored and no changes are to be made in the scores of other yachts, except that, when the incident from which the penalty resulted occurred in a particular race, she shall be disqualified from that race and the yachts *finishing* behind her in that race shall each be moved up one place.

(c) When a scoring system provides that one or more scores are to be excluded in calculating a yacht's total score, a disqualification under Fundamental Rule C, Fair Sailing, Fundamental Rule D, Accepting Penalties, or rule 54, Propulsion, shall not be excluded.

74.6 THE DECISION

(a) After making its decision, the **protest committee** shall promptly communicate the following to the **parties to the protest:**

  (i) the facts found,

  (ii) the **rule** or **rules** judged applicable,

  (iii) the decision and grounds on which it is based,

  (iv) the yacht or yachts penalised, if any, and

(v)   the penalty imposed, if any, or the redress granted, if any.

(b) A **party to the protest** shall on request be supplied with:

   (i)   the above details in writing, and

   (ii)   unless irrelevant, a diagram of the incident endorsed by the **protest committee.**

SECTION C—Special Rules

75   Gross Infringement of Rules or Misconduct

75.1 PENALTIES BY THE RACE COMMITTEE OR PROTEST COMMITTEE

(a) The race committee or **protest committee** may call a hearing when it has reasonable grounds for believing that a competitor has committed a gross infringement of the **rules** or a gross breach of good manners or sportmanship.

(b) When the **protest committee** finds that there has been a gross infringement of the **rules** or a gross breach of good manners or sportsmanship, it may exclude a competitor, and a yacht when appropriate, either from further participation in a series, or from the whole series, or take other disciplinary action. The committee shall report any penalty imposed to its national authority, and to that of the competitor, and to that of the yacht.

(c) No action shall be taken under this rule without a written statement of allegation and a hearing held in accordance with the rules of Section B, Protest Procedure.

(d) Any hearing under this rule shall be conducted by a **protest committee** consisting of at least three members.

75.2 PENALTIES BY THE NATIONAL AUTHORITY
Upon a receipt of a report of gross infringement of the **rules** or a gross breach of good manners or sportsmanship, or a report of a penalty imposed under rule 75.1, a national authority may conduct an investigation and, when appropriate, a hearing and take such action as it deems appropriate against the person or persons or the yacht involved. Such action may include disqualification from participating in any race held in its jurisdiction for any period, or other disciplinary action. The national authority shall report any penalty imposed to the national authority of the competitor, and to that of the yacht, and to the International Yacht Racing Union. The IYRU shall inform all national authorities, which may also apply a penalty.

76   Liability

76.1 DAMAGES
The question of damages arising from an infringement of any of the **rules** shall be governed by the prescriptions, if any, of the national authority.

76.2 MEASUREMENT EXPENSES
Unless otherwise prescribed by the **protest committee,** the fees and expenses entailed by a **protest** on measurement or classification shall be paid by the unsuccessful party.

SECTION D—Appeals

77   **Right of Appeal and Decisions**

77.1   RIGHT OF APPEAL

Except when the right of appeal has been denied in accordance with rule 1.5(a) or (b), Right of Appeal, a **party to a protest** may appeal a decision of a **protest committee** to the national authority concerned. A race committee that is a **party to a protest** may appeal only the decision of an independent protest committee or jury.

77.2   RIGHT OF REFERENCE

A **protest committee** may refer its own decision to the national authority for confirmation or correction of its interpretation of the **rules**. A reference shall contain the **protest committee's** decision and the relevant documents listed in rule 78.1(b), (Appellant's Responsibilities).

77.3   QUESTIONS OF INTERPRETATION

When no **protest** that may be appealed is involved, a national authority may answer questions from a club or other organisation affiliated to it. A question shall contain sufficient detail for an interpretation to be made.

77.4   INTERPRETATION OF RULES

Appeals, references and questions shall be made only on interpretations of the **rules**. The national authority shall accept the **protest committee's** finding of facts, except that, when it is not satisfied with the facts presented, it may request further information from the **protest committee** or return the **protest** for a re-hearing.

77.5   INTERESTED PARTIES

No **interested party** or member of the **protest committee** shall take any part in the discussion or decision upon an appeal or reference.

77.6   DECISIONS

(a)   A national authority may uphold, reverse or alter a **protest committee's** decision. When, from the facts found by the **protest committee**, it believes that any yacht that was a **party to the protest** infringed a **rule**, it shall penalise her, irrespective of whether that yacht or that **rule** was mentioned in the decision.

(b)   The decision of the national authority shall be final, and shall be transmitted in writing by the national authority to all **parties to the protest** and the **protest committee,** who shall be bound by the decision.

78   **Appeal Procedures**

78.1   APPELLANT'S RESPONSIBILITIES

(a)   Within 15 days of receiving the **protest committee's** written decision or its decision not to re-open a hearing, the appellant shall transmit to the national authority the dated appeal, which shall include the grounds for the appeal, i.e. why the appellant believes the **protest committee's** interpretation of the **rules** to be incorrect, and a copy of the **protest committee's** decision.

(b)   Any of the following documents in the appellant's possession shall be sent with the appeal or as soon as possible thereafter:

(i)   the protest form(s);

(ii)   a diagram, prepared or endorsed by the **protest committee**, showing the force and direction of the wind; the set and rate of the current or tidal stream, if any; the course to the next *mark*, or the *mark* itself, and the required side; the positions and tracks of all yachts involved; and, if relevant, the depth of the water;

(iii)   the notice of race, the sailing instructions, any other conditions governing the event, and any amendments thereto;

(iv)   any written statements submitted by the **parties to the protest** to the **protest committee**;

(v)   any additional relevant documents; and

(vi)   the names and addresses of all **parties to the protest** and the protest committee chairman.

78.2 NOTIFICATION OF THE PROTEST COMMITTEE
Upon receipt of a valid appeal, the national authority shall transmit a copy of the appeal to the **protest committee,** informing the **protest committee** of the documents supplied by the appellant.

78.3 PROTEST COMMITTEE'S RESPONSIBILITIES
The **protest committee** shall transmit to the national authority the documents listed in rule 78.1(b) that were not supplied by the appellant. The **protest committee** shall include any comments on the appeal that it may wish to make.

78.4 NATIONAL AUTHORITY'S RESPONSIBILITIES
The national authority shall transmit copies of the appeal and any other relevant documents to the other **parties to the protest.** It shall transmit to the appellant copies of documents that were not supplied by the appellant.

78.5 COMMENTS
All **parties to the protest** may submit comments on the appeal to the national authority within a reasonable time, and at the same time shall transmit copies of such documents to the other **parties to the protest** and the **protest committee**.

78.6 FEE
A national authority may prescribe that a fee be paid for it to consider an appeal, reference or question, and shall allow a reasonable time for payment.

78 7 WITHDRAWING AN APPEAL
An appellant may withdraw an appeal by accepting the decision of the **protest committee**.

APPENDIX 1—Definition of an Amateur and Eligibility Regulations

1   Amateur

1.1   For the purpose of international yacht races in which yachts are required to have one or more amateurs on board and in other races with similar requirements, an amateur is a yachtsman who engages in yacht racing as a pastime as distinguished from a means of obtaining a livelihood or part-time compensation other than that permitted by the Guidelines to the Eligibility Code. No yachtsman shall lose amateur status by reason of his livelihood being derived from designing or constructing yachts, yacht parts, sails or accessories; or from similar professions associated with the sport; or solely from the maintenance (but not the *racing*) of yachts.

1.2   Competing in a race in which a prize is offered having a value greater than US$300, other than a prize awarded only for temporary possession, is ground for loss of amateur status unless prior to the event:

   (i)   the competitor assigns to the IYRU, his national authority or his national Olympic committee all his rights to such prize, or

   (ii)   the organising authority obtains its national authority's consent to a prize having a value greater than US$300.

1.3   Any yachtsman whose amateur status is questioned or is in doubt may apply to his national authority for recognition of his amateur status. Any such applicant may be required to provide such particulars and evidence and to pay such fees as the national authority may prescribe. Recognition may be suspended or cancelled by the national authority granting it, and, upon application by the competitor affected, the authority may reinstate recognition of amateur status following a period of at least two years absence from the sport.

1.4   The Permanent Committee of the IYRU or any tribunal nominated by the chairman of that committee may review the decision of any national authority affecting the amateur status of a yachtsman for the purpose of competing in international races.

2   I.O.C. Rule 26 - Eligibility Code

To be eligible for participation in the Olympic Games, a competitor must:

   —   observe and abide by the Rules of the International Olympic Committee (IOC) and in addition the rules of his or her International Federation (IF), as approved by the IOC, even if the Federation's rules are more strict than those of the IOC;

   —   not have received any financial rewards or material benefit in connection with his or her sports participation, except as permitted in the bye-laws to this rule.

BYE-LAWS TO RULE 26

A.   Each IF is responsible for the wording of the eligibility code relating to its sport, which must be approved by the Executive Board in the name of the IOC.

B.   The observation of Rule 26 and of the eligibility codes of IFs are under the responsibility of IFs and National Olympic Committee (NOC) involved. The Eligibility Commission of the IOC will ensure the application of these provisions.

C.   All cases of infringement of Rule 26 of the IOC and of the eligibility codes of IFs shall be communicated by the respective IF or NOC to the IOC to be taken in consideration by its eligibility commission. In accordance with Rule 23 and its bye-law, the accused competitor may request to be heard by the Executive Board whose decision will be final.

GUIDELINES TO ELIGIBILITY CODE FOR THE IFs

A.   The following regulations are based on the principle that an athlete's health must not suffer nor must he or she be placed at a social or material disadvantage as a result of his or her preparation for and participation in the Olympic Games and international sports competitions. In accordance with Rule 26, the IOC, the IFs, the NOCs, and the National Authorities will assume responsibility for the protection and support of athletes.

B.   All competitors, men or women, who conform to the criteria set out in Rule 26, may participate in the Olympic Games, except those who have:

1.   been registered as professional athletes or professional coaches in any sport. Each National Authority shall provide a means for registering professional yachtsmen and women, and professional coaches. In this connection:

(a)   Professional yachtsmen or women shall be persons who do not comply with the definition of an amateur as defined in Appendix 1 of the current Yacht Racing Rules.

(b)   Professional coaches shall be persons who obtain their principal means of livelihood from teaching the skills of yacht racing.

2.   signed a contract as a professional athlete or professional coach in any sport before the official closing of the Olympic Games.

3.   accepted without the knowledge of their IF, National Authority or NOC a material advantage for their preparation or participation in yachting competition except:

(a)   either from, or with the permission of their National Authority; or

(b)   from funds held by the National Authority however obtained which are being held by that Authority or Trust for or on behalf of either an individual or class of yachtsmen.

(c)   National Authorities may issue guidelines for the receipt of such material advantages which shall cover:

(i)   Reimbursement of expenses properly incurred in preparation for, and competing in an international or Olympic event.

(ii)   The provision of equipment for such events.

(iii)   Living and accommodation allowances and including allowances in lieu of normal salary, etc., if the same is lost due to the yachtsman engaging in such preparation or competition.

(d)   The receipt of money as a prize, or otherwise, not exceeding US$300 shall not be a breach of this clause.

4.   allowed their person, name, picture, or sports performances to be used for advertising, except when their IF, NOC or National Authority has entered into a contract for sponsorship or equipment. All payment must be made to the IF, NOC or National Authority concerned, and not to the athlete.

5.   carried advertising material on their person or clothing in the Olympic Games and Games under the patronage of the IOC, other than trademarks on technical equipment or clothing as agreed by the IOC with the IFs.

In the absence of any special agreement by the IOC with the IF's, advertising material on clothing shall not exceed that on clothing commercially available to the public *provided however* that only one maker's mark may be displayed on clothing worn by yachtsmen and provided that such a mark shall fit within a square not exceeding 100mm by 100mm.

6.   in the practice of sport and in the opinion of the IOC, manifestly contravened the spirit of fair play in the exercise of sport, particularly by the use of doping or violence.

APPENDIX 2 — Sailboard Racing Rules

Sailboard races shall be *sailed* under the International Yacht Racing Rules modified as follows:

1   Part I - Definitions

1.1   *Leeward and Windward* - The *windward* side of a sailboard is the side that is, or, when head to wind or with the wind astern, was, towards the wind, regardless of the direction in which the sailboard is *sailing*. However, when *sailing* by the lee (i.e. with the wind coming over her stern from the stern from the same side as her boom is on) the *windward* side is the other side. The opposite side is the *leeward* side.

When neither of two sailboards on the same *tack* is *clear astern*, the one on the *windward* side of the other is the *windward sailboard*. The other is the *leeward sailboard*.

1.2   *Capsized* and *Recovering*

(a)   *Capsized*—A sailboard is *capsized* when she is not under way due to her sail being is the water or when the competitor is waterstarting.

(b)   *Recovering*—A sailboard is *recovering* from a *capsize* from the time her sail or, when waterstarting, the competitor's body is raised out of the water until she has steerage way.

2   Part III - General Requirements

2.1   Rule 19.1 - Measurement or Rating Certificates

When so prescribed by the national authority, a numbered and dated device on the board, daggerboard and sail shall rank as a measurement certificate.

2.2   Rule 23 - Anchor

An anchor and chain or rope need not be carried.

2.3   Rule 24 - Life Saving Equipment

A safety device shall prevent the mast separating from the board.

2.4   Rule 25 - Class Insignia, National Letters and Sail Numbers

Rule 25.1(a) - The class insignia shall be displayed once on each side of the sail. It shall fit within a rectangle of 0.5 m², the longer dimension of which shall not exceed one metre. It shall not refer to anything other than the manufacturer or class and shall not consist of more than two letters and three numbers. When approved by the IYRU or a national authority within its jurisdiction, this insignia shall not be considered to be advertising.

3   Part IV - Right of Way Rules

3.1   Rule 33 - Contact between Yachts Racing

As between each other, rule 33 shall not apply to sailboards.

3.2   Rule 38.2(a) - Proper Course Limitations
Rule 40 - Same Tack - Luffing before Clearing the Starting Line

For "mainmast" read "foot of mast".

3.3   Rule 46 - Person Overboard; Yacht Anchored; Aground or Capsized

Rule 46.3 does not apply.

3.4   Recovering from a Capsize

A sailboard *recovering* from a *capsize* shall not obstruct a sailboard or yacht under way.

3.5   Sail out of the Water when Starting

When approaching the starting line to *start*, a sailboard shall have her sail out of the water and in a normal position, except when *capsized* unintentionally.

3.6   Sailing Backward when Starting

When approaching the starting line to *start* or when on the course side of the starting line, a sailboard *sailing* or drifting backward shall keep clear of other sailboards and yachts.

4   Part V - Other Sailing Rules

Rule 54 - Propulsion

Dragging a foot in the water to check way is permissible. In rule 54.3(b), for "sheet" read "wishbone", and delete the last sentence.

5   Part VI - Protests, Penalties and Appeals

Rule 68 - Protests by Yachts

A sailboard need not display a flag in order to signify her intention to protest as required by rule 68.3, but, except when rule 68.4 applies, she shall try to notify the other sailboard or yacht by hail at the first reasonable opportunity and the race committee as soon as possible after *finishing* or retiring.

6   APPENDIX 3 - Alternative Penalties for Infringement of a Rule of Part IV

6.1   720° Turns

Unless otherwise prescribed in the sailing instructions, the 720° Turns penalty in Appendix 3.1 shall apply. Two full 360° turns of the board shall satisfy the provision of the 720° Turns penalty.

6.2   Percentage

A sailboard need not display Code flag "I" to acknowledge an infringement. She shall notify the other sailboard or yacht by hail immediately and the race committee as soon as possible after *finishing* or retiring.

7   Rules for Multi-Mast Sailboards

7.1   Part IV - Rule 38.2(a) and Rule 40

The normal station of the helmsman is the normal station of the crew member controlling the mainsail. The mainsail is the foremost sail and the mainmast is the foremost mast.

7.2   Appendix 2 - Rule 1.2(a) *Capsized*

A multi-mast sailboard is *capsized* when one or more of her sails are in the water or one or more competitors are waterstarting.

7.3   Appendix 2 - Rule 1.2(b) *Recovering*

A multi-mast sailboard is *recovering* from a *capsize* from the time her sails or, when waterstarting, the competitors' bodies are raised out of the water until she has steerage way.

7.3   Appendix 2 - Rule 3.4 - Sail out of the Water when Starting

For "sail" read "sails".

Funboard Racing Rules

These rules apply for alternative sailboard races only, i.e. course races and slalom, but not for triangle (Olympic course) races. Funboard races, both course races and slalom, shall be *sailed* under the International Yacht Racing Rules, Appendix 2, modified as follows:

A. **The following rules apply for both Course Races and Slalom.**

8 **Part V - Other Sailing Rules**

8.1 Rule 52 - Touching a Mark

Rules 52.1(a)(ii) and (iii) do not apply.

8.2 Rule 54 - Propulsion

Rule 54 is replaced by: "A sailboard shall be propelled by the action of the wind on the sail, by the action of the water on the hull and by the unassisted actions of the competitor."

9 **Part VI - Protests, Penalties and Appeals**

9.1 Rule 68 - Protests by Yachts

A **protest** does not need to be in writing but may be made orally.

9.2 Rule 77 - Right of Appeal and Decisions

Except for a competitor or sailboard penalised under rule 75.1, Gross Infringement of Rules or Misconduct, the right of appeal is denied.

B. **The following rules apply for Slalom only.**

10 **Part I - Definitions**

10.1 *Going Out* and *Coming In* - when *sailing* from the shore against the incoming surf, a sailboard is *going out*. A sailboard *sailing* in the opposite direction is *coming in*.

10.2 *Overtaking* - A sailboard is *overtaking* from the moment she establishes an *overlap* from *clear astern* until she is *clear ahead* of the overtaken sailboard. When an *overlap* exists at the preparatory signal, the *windward sailboard* shall be deemed to be overtaking.

11 **Part II - Organisation and Management**

Rule 6 - Starting and Finishing Lines

The starting and finishing lines may be positioned on the shore.

12 **Part IV - Right of Way Rules**

12.1 Except for rule 37.2, rules 36 to 42 do not apply.

12.2 Basic Rules

(a) A sailboard *coming in* shall keep clear of a sailboard *going out*.

(b) When neither *going out* nor *coming in*, a *port-tack* sailboard shall keep clear of a *starboard-tack* sailboard.

12.3 Changing Tacks - Tacking and Gybing

Except when *gybing* around a *mark*, a sailboard that is *tacking* or *gybing* shall keep clear of a sailboard *on a tack*.

12.4 Same Tack - Overtaking

An *overtaking* sailboard shall keep clear of the overtaken sailboard.

APPENDIX 3 - Alternative Penalties for Infringement of a Rule of Part IV

Experience indicates that the 720° turns penalty is most satisfactory for small boats in relatively short races, but that it can be dangerous for large yachts and in restricted waters and not sufficiently severe in long races. The 20% penalty is relatively mild and is designed to encourage acknowledgement of infringements and willingness to protest when not acknowledged. Both systems keep yachts *racing*.

Either of the following alternatives to disqualification may be used by including in the sailing instructions a provision such as the following (or if preferred the selected penalty may be quoted in full):

"The 720° Turns penalty, Appendix 3.1 (or the Percentage penalty, Appendix 3.2) of the racing rules will apply."

1   720° Turns

1.1   A yacht that may have infringed a rule of Part IV may accept an alternative penalty by *sailing* well clear of all other yachts as soon as possible after the incident, and remaining clear while she makes two complete 360° turns (720°) in the same direction, including two *tacks* and two *gybes*.

1.2   When the infringement occurs at the finishing line, she shall make her turns on the course side of the line before she will be recorded as having *finished*.

1.3   A yacht intending to protest shall hail the other yacht immediately and act in accordance with rule 68, Protests by Yachts. A yacht that accepts an alternative penalty may protest with respect to the same incident. She shall not be penalised further for an infringement for which she accepted the penalty, except as provided by paragraph 1.4.

1.4   The **protest committee** may disqualify a yacht that has accepted an alternative penalty when it finds that her infringement resulted in serious damage or that she gained a significant advantage.

1.5   Failure to accept an alternative penalty will make an infringing yacht liable to disqualification or other prescribed penalty. When a yacht complies with some but not all of the requirements of paragraphs 1.1 or 1.2, the yacht infringed against is relieved of further obligations under rule 33, Contact between Yachts Racing.

2   Percentage

2.1   A yacht that may have infringed a rule of Part IV may accept an alternative penalty:

    (a)   by displaying Code flag "I" at the first reasonable opportunity after the incident, and

    (b)   except for a yacht *sailed* single-handed, by keeping it displayed until she has *finished*, and

    (c)   by reporting her acknowledgement and the yacht infringed against to the race committee immediately after *finishing*.

She shall receive a score for the place worse than her actual finishing position by 20% of the number of starters*, but not less than three places, calculated in accordance with paragraph 2.7.

2.2 A yacht intending to protest shall hail the other yacht immediately and act in accordance with rule 68, Protests by Yachts. A yacht that accepts an alternative penalty may protest with respect to the same incident; however, her penalty shall not be affected. She shall not be penalised further for an infringement for which she accepted the penalty, except as provided by paragraph 2.5.

2.3 A yacht may protest without displaying a protest flag against a yacht that has complied with some but not all of the requirements of paragraph 2.1.

2.4 A yacht that does not comply with the requirements of paragraph 2.1, but acknowledges an infringement prior to a hearing, shall be penalised 50%, but not less than six places.

2.5 The **protest committee** may disqualify a yacht that has accepted an alternative penalty when it finds that her infringement resulted in serious damage or that she gained a significant advantage.

2.6 Failure to accept an alternative penalty will make an infringing yacht liable to disqualification or other prescribed penalty. When a yacht complies with some but not all of the requirements of paragraph 2.1, the yacht infringed against is relieved of further obligations under rule 33, Contact between Yachts Racing. A yacht may request a hearing solely on the point of having complied with the requirements of paragraph 2.1.

2.7 The penalty shall be computed as 20% (or 50%) of the number of starters* in the event to the nearest whole number (round .5 upward), such number to be not less than three (or six), except that a yacht shall not receive a score worse than for one position more than the number of starters*. (Examples: an infringing yacht finishing 8th in a start for 19 yachts would receive a score for 12th place: 8 + (19 x 20% = 3.8 or 4) = 12. Another infringing yacht, finishing 18th, would receive the score for 20th place.) The imposition of a percentage penalty shall not affect the scores of other yachts. Thus, two yachts may receive the same score.

2.8 A yacht infringing a rule in more than one incident shall receive a penalty for each incident.

* When scoring a regatta, these calculations shall be based on the number of yachts entered in the series, not the number of starters in the race in question.

APPENDIX 4—Team Racing and Match Racing Rules

SECTION A—Team Racing Rules

Team racing shall be *sailed* under the International Yacht Racing Rules supplemented and altered as follows:

1   Sailing Rules

1.1   Except when *sailing* a *proper course*, a yacht shall not act to interfere with another yacht *sailing* on a different leg of the course. Each time a leg is *sailed*, it is a different leg.

1.2   Right of way may be waived between team-mate yachts, provided that doing so does not directly affect a yacht of the other team adversely.

1.3   When contact occurs between team-mate yachts and neither promptly displays a green flag, rule 33, Contact between Yachts Racing, will apply, except that only the lower-scoring yacht shall receive the penalty points prescribed in paragraph 3.4(c). A yacht disabled by a team-mate yacht is ineligible for redress under rule 69(c), Requests for Redress.

1.4   Except to protect her position or that of a team-mate yacht, a yacht that is *sailing* the last leg of the course shall not act to interfere with a yacht of another team that has no opponent astern of her. A team-mate yacht shall not attempt to render this rule inapplicable by reducing speed or departing from a *proper course*.

1.5   Rule 41.3, Onus, does not apply.

1.6   A yacht that receives assistance from a team-mate yacht does not infringe rule 60, Outside Assistance.

2   Acknowledgement of Infringements; Intention to Protest

2.1   A yacht may acknowledge an infringement of a rule of Part IV, except rule 32, Serious Damage, by hailing such acknowledgement to the yacht infringed against immediately, and by promptly displaying a green flag. After displaying the flag, she shall not remove it. She shall display one green flag for each incident, unless all green flags supplied are already displayed.

2.2   A yacht intending to protest shall hail the other yacht immediately and promptly display a red flag. She shall display one red flag for each incident, unless all red flags supplied are already displayed. A yacht that has displayed a red flag and that decides reasonably promptly thereafter that she, and not the other yacht, was at fault shall immediately replace the red flag with a green flag and hail the other yacht accordingly.

2.3   When a yacht displaying a red flag with respect to an incident is satisfied that the other yacht has displayed a green flag in accordance with paragraph 2.1 or 2.2, she shall immediately remove her red flag.

3   Scoring a Race

3.1   Each yacht *finishing* a race shall score three-quarters of a point for first place, two points for second place, three points for third place, and so on. A yacht that does not *start*, *finish* or *sail* the course shall receive points equal to the number of yachts entitled to *race*. Each yacht, including one that retires, shall also receive penalty points as provided in paragraph 3.4. The team with the lower total points wins.

3.2   When all yachts of one team have *finished* or retired, the race committee may stop the race. Other yachts still *racing* shall receive the points they would have scored had they *finished*.

3.3 When all the yachts of a team forfeit or fail to *start* in a race, each shall receive points equal to the number of yachts entitled to *race*, and the yachts of the other team shall be scored as if they had *finished* in the best positions.

3.4 In addition to the points prescribed above, a yacht shall receive penalty points as follows:

Infringement	Penalty Points
(a) An infringement of a rule of Part IV, other than rule 32, acknowledged in accordance with paragraph 2.1.	2.5
(b) Failure to *start*, *finish* or *sail* the course.	2.5
(c) An infringement of any **rule**, other than rule 32, not acknowledged in accordance with paragraph 2.1.	6
(d) An infringement of rule 32.	10

When a yacht gains a significant advantage from an infringement of a rule of Part IV that was acknowledged in accordance with paragraph 2.1, she may be further penalised.

4   Scoring a Series

4.1 A team racing series shall consist of races or matches. A match shall consist of two races between the same two teams. The team with the lower total points for the race or the match shall be the winner.

4.2 When two or more teams are competing in a series consisting of races or matches, the series winner shall be the team winning the greatest number of races or matches. The other teams shall be ranked in order of number of wins. Tied matches shall count as one-half win to each team.

4.3 When there is a tie:

(a) Ties between two teams will be broken in favour of the winner of the match or race when the two teams met, or, failing this, the winner of the second race of that match.

(b) Ties between three or more teams will be broken in favour of the team or teams scoring the lowest aggregate points when the tied teams met, or, failing this, the lowest total points in the series. Failing this, the tie shall be broken by drawing lots.

When Organising Authorities Supply All Yachts

5   Assignment of Yachts

5.1 The organising authority shall form groups of yachts, and for the first race shall draw lots to assign the groups to the teams. The groups of yachts shall be exchanged between races so that, in so far as possible, each team uses each group the same number of times. The organising authority shall identify each yacht within her group by use of special sail numbers or by display of a distinctive colour in her rigging or on her hull or sails.

5.2 In a two-team series after an even number of races, either team may require that the yachts be re-grouped. The groups will be assigned for the next race by the spin of a coin, except that, when there will be a final odd race in a series between a host team and a visiting team, the visiting team shall choose the group it will use.

5.3 Sails and other equipment shall remain with a yacht throughout the event, except when damage or loss requires the race committee to make substitutions. In such case, it shall inform all teams affected thereby.

6 Breakdowns

6.1 A yacht suffering a breakdown shall display a red flag as soon as practicable and, when possible, continue *racing*.

6.2 When the race committee decides that the yacht's finishing position was materially prejudiced, that the breakdown was not the fault of the crew, and that in the circumstances a reasonably competent crew would not have been able to avoid the material prejudice, it shall make as equitable a decision as possible, which may be to order the race to be re-sailed, or, when the yacht's finishing position was predictable, award her points for that position. In case of doubt as to her position when she broke down, the doubt shall be resolved against her.

6.3 A breakdown caused by defective equipment, or by an infringement by an opponent, shall not normally be deemed to be the fault of the crew, but one caused by careless handling, capsizing or by an infringement by a yacht of the same team shall be. When in doubt about the fault of the crew, the race committee shall resolve it in the yacht's favour.

SECTION B—Match Racing Rules

Match racing shall be *sailed* under the International Yacht Racing Rules as altered by this appendix. A match is a race between two yachts. The sailing instructions may prescribe that parts of the appendix will not apply or make further alterations in accordance with rule 3.1, Sailing Instructions.

1 Alterations to the Racing Rules

1.1 Rule 32 is altered to read: "A right-of-way yacht shall attempt to avoid a collision resulting in damage."

1.2 Rule 39 is altered to read: "A yacht that is on a free leg of the course shall not *sail* below her *proper course* when she is clearly within three of her overall lengths of a *leeward yacht.*"

1.3 Rules 64.2 and 64.3 are altered to read: "A spinnaker may be set without a boom. When a spinnaker boom is used, it shall be carried only on the side of the mast opposite to the main boom and shall be fixed to the mast, except when shifting it or the sail attached to it."

2   Further Alterations to the Rules when Umpiring (On-the-water judging) is used

2.1   Fundamental Rule D - Add: "A yacht may wait for the umpires' decision before taking a penalty."

2.2   Rule 33 does not apply.

2.3   Rule 38.2(c) is altered to read: "When there is doubt, the *leeward yacht* may assume that she has the right to *luff* or *sail* above her *proper course* unless the *windward yacht* has made an audible sound signal. The *leeward yacht* shall be governed by such a signal."

2.4   Rules 41.3, 42.1(c) and (d), and 43.2(b)(iii) do not apply.

2.5   In so far as the provisions of match racing rule 5 conflict with the rules of Part VI, Part VI does not apply.

3   Additional Right of Way Rules

3.1   A yacht shall not act to interfere with:

(a)   a yacht on another leg of the course, or

(b)   a yacht in another match, or

(c)   a penalised yacht that is getting clear and while she is exonerating herself.

3.2   A yacht that is exonerating herself shall keep clear of the other yacht until she has completed her penalty and is on a *proper course* to the next *mark*.

3.3   When umpiring is being used, infringements of this rule will be signalled in accordance with rule 5.2(c).

4   Pre-Start Procedure

4.1   Before her preparatory signal, a yacht shall proceed to and remain outside the end of the starting line assigned to her.

4.2   Within the two-minute period following her preparatory signal, a yacht shall cross the starting line from the course side to the pre-start side, and shall keep clear of any yachts *racing* in a preceding match until she is wholly on the pre-start side.

4.3   Infringement of this rule is not open to protest by a yacht.

5   Umpiring, Protest Procedure, Penalties

5.1   UMPIRES
For a match racing event where decisions are to be made on the water, umpires who have an intimate knowledge of the **rules** and are experienced in judging match races shall be appointed. Umpires may serve on the jury appointed to hear **protests** arising under rule 5.5(e).

5.2 PROTESTS ALLEGING INFRINGEMENT OF A RIGHT OF WAY RULE
For **protests** alleging infringements of the rules of Sections B and C of Part IV, Sections A and B of Part VI are modified as follows:

(a) An umpires' vessel with at least two umpires aboard will be assigned to each match.

(b) When a yacht considers that the other yacht has infringed a rule of Sections B and C of Part IV, she may protest by immediately and conspicuously displaying Code flag "Y" from her backstay (or shroud when no backstay) and hailing "Protest".

(c) As soon as possible thereafter, the umpires will decide whether either or both yachts have infringed such a rule. The umpires will immediately inform both yachts of their decision by displaying a visual signal accompanied by a sound signal as follows:

   (i) A green flag means: "No infringement";

   (ii) A placard identifying a yacht means: "The designated yacht has infringed a rule, is penalised and shall exonerate herself in accordance with rule 5.2(e)".

(d) The protesting yacht shall lower Code flag "Y" as soon as possible after the umpires' signal.

(e) Unless otherwise prescribed in the sailing instructions, the penalised yacht shall *sail* clear of the other yacht and do a 270° turn, including a *gybe*. When the penalty is signalled:

   (i) before the starting signal, it shall be done as soon as possible after *starting*.

   (ii) on a windward leg, it shall be done as soon as possible.

   (iii) on a free leg, it shall be done as soon as possible after commencing the next windward leg.

(f) When the umpires fail to make a signal required by rule 5.2(c):

   (i) a protested yacht may acknowledge the infringement by taking the penalty prescribed under rule 5.2(e);

   (ii) when no penalty is taken with respect to that protest, the umpires may act in accordance with rule 5.5(b) or (e).

5.3 NON-ACCEPTABLE PROTESTS
A yacht shall not protest the other yacht for an alleged infringement of the rules of Section A of Part IV, or rule 52, Touching a Mark, or rule 54, Propulsion.

5.4 ACTION BY UMPIRES
When the umpires decide that a yacht:

(a) has failed to comply with rule 5.2, or

(b) has infringed rule 52, Touching a Mark, or rule 54, Propulsion, or

(c) has caused damage to either yacht, or

(d) after completing her penalty, has gained an advantage over the other yacht.

they may penalise the yacht in accordance with rules 5.2(c) and (e) or disqualify the yacht and terminate the match. Such disqualification and termination will be signalled by the display of a black flag with the placard designating the penalised yacht.

5.5 PROTESTS BASED ON OTHER RULES AND REQUESTS FOR REDRESS

(a) A yacht can protest another yacht for an alleged infringement of a sailing instruction or a **rule** other than those specified in rules 5.2 and 5.3, or can request redress in accordance with racing rule 69, Requests for Redress. Such a **protest** shall be signalled by displaying Code flag "B" or a rectangular red flag conspicuously from her backstay (or shroud if no backstay) until acknowledged by the umpires or the race committee.

(b) Following the race, the umpires will take testimony in any way they deem appropriate, and may make a decision that may be communicated orally.

(c) The umpires may act independently and may decide that a yacht has infringed a sailing instruction or **rule** other than those specified in rules 5.2 and 5.4, and may communicate the decision orally.

(d) When the umpires decide that a yacht has infringed a **rule** that has had no significant effect on the outcome of the match, a penalty of one-third of a point may be imposed.

(e) When the umpires deem it more appropriate to conduct a hearing ashore, or to re-open or resume a hearing held at sea, the yachts will be advised and a jury appointed that will proceed in accordance with the rules of Part VI.

5.6 APPEALS
There shall be no appeals from decisions or re-opening of decisions made in accordance with rules 5.2 and 5.4.

6 Scoring

6.1 Points are awarded to yachts, except that when yachts are interchanged, the points are awarded to helmsmen. The winner of each match scores one point, the loser scores no points. The winner is the one with the most points at the end of a series. When there is a round robin series (in which each races against all the others), and then a semi-final or final series, points from each series are not carried forward to the next.

6.2 A yacht that has won a match but is disqualified for an infringement against a yacht in another match shall lose the point for that match. However, the losing yacht shall not be awarded the point.

6.3 A two-way tie in a round robin series shall be decided by the result of the match between the tied yachts. When possible, this principle shall be applied when more than two are tied.

6.4 When rule 6.3 does not resolve a tie, it shall, when practicable, be resolved by a sail-off or otherwise in a manner prescribed by the race committee.

APPENDIX 5—Scoring Systems

The two scoring systems most often used are the Olympic and the Low-Point. The Olympic system has been adopted for many class championships; the Low-Point system is suitable both for championships and for club and other small fleet racing, and is somewhat easier to use for race committees and competitors.

In both systems, lower points designate better finishing places. The Low-Point system uses a 'straight line' points schedule that rewards performance in direct proportion to finishing place; the Olympic system uses a "curved" points schedule that provides an additional reward in the top six finishing places. Although designed primarily for scoring regattas, either system may be used for other series; see paragraph 3, Suggested Alterations for Non-Regatta Series.

The sailing instructions may include a complete system verbatim or may incorporate either system by reference, with or without alterations, as explained in the notes following each system. See also Appendix 12, Sailing Instructions Guide, Instruction 18.

1 The Olympic Scoring System

1.1 NUMBER OF RACES, MINIMUM REQUIRED, AND RACES TO COUNT
There will be seven races, of which five shall be completed to constitute a series. Each yacht's total score will be the sum of her scores for all races, excluding her worst score in accordance with rule 74.5(c), Points and Places. The lowest total score wins.

1.2 POINTS
Each yacht *finishing* in a race and not thereafter retiring or being disqualified will be scored points as follows:

Finishing Place	Points
First	0
Second	3
Third	5.7
Fourth	8
Fifth	10
Sixth	11.7
Seventh and thereafter	Place plus six

All other yachts, including a yacht that *finishes* and thereafter retires or is disqualified, will be scored points for the finishing place one more than the number of yachts entered in the series.

1.3 TIES
When there is a tie on total points between two or more yachts, the tie will be broken in favour of the yacht or yachts with the most first places, and, when the tie remains, the most second places, and so on, if necessary, for such races as count for total points. When the tie still remains, it shall stand as part of the final results.

Notes: (a) The sailing instructions can incorporate the Olympic system by stating "The Olympic Scoring System, Appendix 5.1 of the racing rules, will apply."

(b) When the number of races is not seven, add "except that ___ races are scheduled, of which __ shall be completed to constitute a series." (Insert the numbers of races.)

(c) When all races are to be counted, add "except that each yacht's total score will be the sum of her scores for all races."

2 The Low-Point Scoring System

2.1 NUMBER OF RACES, MINIMUM REQUIRED, AND RACES TO COUNT

The number of races scheduled and the number required to constitute a series shall be prescribed in the sailing instructions. Each yacht's total score will be the sum of her scores for all races, excluding her worst score in accordance with rule 74.5(c), Points and Places. The lowest total score wins.

2.2 POINTS

Each yacht *finishing* in a race and not thereafter retiring or being disqualified will be scored points equal to her finishing place, minus one-quarter point for first place, as follows:

Finishing Place	Points
First	3/4
Second	2
Third	3
Fourth	4
and so on.	

All other yachts, including a yacht that *finishes* and thereafter retires or is disqualified, will be scored points for the finishing place one more than the number of yachts entered in the series.

2.3 TIES

When there is a tie on total points between two or more yachts, the tie will be broken in favour of the yacht or yachts with the most first places, and, when the tie remains, the most second places, and so on, if necessary, for such races as count for total points. When the tie still remains, it shall stand as part of the final results.

Notes:(d) The sailing instructions can incorporate the Low-Point system by stating "The Low-Point Scoring System, Appendix 5.2 of the racing rules, will apply, with __ races scheduled of which __ shall be completed to constitute a series." (Insert the numbers of races.)

(e) When all races are to be counted, add "except that each yacht's total score will be the sum of her scores for all races."

3 Suggested Alterations for Non-Regatta Series

3.1

In a regatta all yachts are expected to compete in all races, and the difference between the number of entrants and the number of starters is usually insignificant. However, in a longer series there may be a number of yachts that compete in fewer races than others, in which case it is suggested that the following be substituted for the last paragraph in either 1.2 or 2.2:

A yacht that does not *start* or rank as a starter in accordance with rule 50, Ranking as a Starter, will be scored points for the finishing place one more than the number of yachts entered in the series. All other yachts, including a yacht that *finishes* but thereafter retires or is disqualified, will be scored points for the finishing place one more than the number of yachts that *started* or ranked as starters in accordance with rule 50 in that race.

3.2   When it is desired to increase the number of races to be excluded from each yacht's series score, change the second sentence in 1.1 or 2.1 to read: "excluding her __ worst scores". (Insert the number.)

4   Guidance for Race and Protest Committees

4.1   ABBREVIATIONS FOR SCORING RECORDS
The following abbreviations are recommended to record the various occurrences that may determine a particular score:

DNC	Did not compete; i.e. did not *start* or rank as a starter under rule 50, Ranking as a Starter.
DNS	Did not *start;* i.e. ranked as a starter under rule 50 but failed to *start.*
PMS	Started prematurely or otherwise failed to comply with the starting procedure.
DNF	Did not *finish.*
RET	Retired after *finishing.*
DSQ	Disqualified.
DND	Disqualification not discardable under rule 74.5(c), Points and Places.
YMP	Yacht materially prejudiced.

4.2   REDRESS
In applying rule 74.2, Consideration of Redress, when it is deemed equitable to adjust the score of the prejudiced yacht by awarding points different from those she received for the race in question, the following possibilities are to be considered:

(i)   Points equal to the average, to the nearest tenth of a point (round .05 upward), of her points in all the races in the series except [her worst race and]* the race in question.

*Delete these words when all scores count for series results, or alter when more than one race is to be excluded.

(ii)   Points equal to the average, to the nearest tenth of a point (round .05 upward), of her points in all the races before the race in question.

(iii)   An arbitrary number of points based on the position of the yacht in the race in question at the time she was prejudiced.

APPENDIX 6—Recommended Protest Committee Procedure

In a protest hearing, the **protest committee** should give equal weight to all testimony; should recognize that honest testimony can vary and even be in conflict as a result of different observations and recollections; should resolve such differences as best it can; should recognize that no yacht is guilty until her infringement has been established to the satisfaction of the **protest committee;** should keep an open mind until all the evidence has been submitted as to whether the protestor or the protestee or a third yacht, when one is involved in the incident, has infringed a **rule.**

1   Preliminaries

1.1   Note on the **protest** the time at which it is received.

1.2   Determine whether the **protest** contains the information called for by rule 68.5, Particulars to be Included, in sufficient detail to identify the incident and the protested yacht, and to tell the recipient what the **protest** is about. If not, ask the protestor to supply the information (rule 68.8, Remedying Defects in the Protest). When a **protest** by a yacht does not identify the nature of the incident, it shall be refused (rules 68.8(a) and 73.2, Acceptance or Refusal of a Protest).

1.3   Unless the **protest** already provides the information;

Inquire whether the protestor displayed a protest flag in accordance with rule 68.3, unless rule 68.4 applies or the protestor is seeking redress under rule 69, and note his answer on the **protest.** When a protest flag has not been properly displayed, the **protest** shall be refused; rule 73.2, Acceptance or Refusal of a Protest, refers, except when the **protest committee** decides either:

(a)   rule 68.4 applies; or

(b)   it was impossible for the yacht to have displayed a protest flag, because she was, for example, dismasted, capsized or sunk.

1.4   Unless the **protest** already provides the information;

Inquire whether the protestor tried to inform the protested yacht(s) (the protestee(s)) that a **protest** would be lodged (rule 68.2, Informing the Protested Yacht) and note his answer on the **protest.** Rule 68.2 is mandatory with regard to the attempt to inform, but not with regard to its success.

See that the protest fee, if any, required by the sailing instructions is included and note its receipt on the **protest** (rule 68.7, Fee).

1.5   When the **protest** conforms to the requirements of rule 68, arrange to hold a hearing as soon as possible. Notify the representative of each yacht involved of the time and place of the hearing (rule 72, Notification of Parties).

1.6   The **protest** and any written statement regarding the incident (preferably photocopies) shall be available to all **parties to the protest** and to the **protest committee** for study before the taking of evidence. A reasonable time shall be allowed for the preparation of defence (rule 72, Notification of Parties).

2   The Hearing

2.1   The **protest committee** shall ensure that:

(a)   a quorum is present as required by the organising authority. The quorum is not affected when it is considered desirable that some members of the **protest committee** leave the hearing during the discussion and decision.

(b)   no **interested party** is a member of the **protest committee** or takes part in the discussion or decision. Ask the **parties to the protest** whether they object to any member on the grounds of "interest". Such an objection shall be made before the **protest** is heard (rule 71.2, Interested Parties).

(c) when any member of the **protest committee** saw the incident, he shall only give his evidence as a witness in the presence of the **parties to the protest** and may be questioned (rule 73.4, Evidence of Committee Member).

(d) when a hearing concerns a request for redress under rule 69, Requests for Redress, or rule 70.3, Yacht Materially Prejudiced, involving a member of the race committee, it is desirable that he is not a member of the **protest committee** and would therefore appear only as a witness.

2.2 The **parties to the protest** or a representative of each (with a language interpreter, when needed) shall have the right to be present throughout the hearing. Each witness, unless he is a member of the **protest committee,** shall be excluded, except when giving his evidence. Others may be admitted as observers at the discretion of the **protest committee** (rule 73.1, Right to be Present).

2.3 Invite first the protestor and then the protestee(s) to give their accounts of the incident. Each may question the other(s). Questions by the **protest committee,** except for clarifying details, are preferably deferred until all accounts have been presented. Models are useful. Positions before and after the incident itself are often helpful.

2.4 Invite first the protestor and then the protestee to call witnesses. They may be questioned by the protestor and protestee as well as by the **protest committee.** The **protest committee** may also call witnesses. It may be appropriate and prudent to ask a witness to disclose any business or other relationship through which he might have an interest or might stand to benefit from the outcome of the **protest.**

2.5 Invite first the protestor and then the protestee to make a final statement of his case, including any application or interpretation of the **rules** to the incident as he sees it.

2.6 The **protest committee** may adjourn a hearing in order to obtain additional evidence.

3 Decision

3.1 The **protest committee,** after dismissing those involved in the incident, shall decide what the relevant facts are (rule 74.1, Finding of Facts).

3.2 The **protest committee** shall then apply the **rules** and reach a decision as to who, if anyone, infringed a **rule** and what **rule** was infringed (rule 74, Decisions and Penalties).

3.3 Having reached a decision in writing, recall the protestor and the protestee and read to them the facts found, the decision and the grounds for it (rule 74.6).

3.4 Any **party to the protest** is entitled to a copy of the decision (rule 74.6), signed by the chairman of the **protest committee.** A copy should also be filed with the committee records.

PROTEST PROCEDURE

	Protest recieved: Date Time Sign		
	Protest flag notices at the finish? ☐ Yes ☐ No		
JURY	☐ No objection about the interested party made		
PRESENT	☐ Protesting yacht represented by:		
	☐ Protested yacht represented by:		
ACCEPTANCE OR REFUSAL	The Protestor		Protest:
	☐ displayed protest flag in accordance with IYRR 68.2		☐ Accepted
	☐ Not displayed a protest flag but IYRR 68.2 applies/a protest flag is not needed for any other reason		☐ Refused because
	☐ immediately informed (when App 3 applies) or tried to inform (in other cases) the protestee		
FACTS FOUND			
RULES applicable			
DECISION and grounds for decision			
CONCLUSION	Signature of Chairman	Decision announced in the presence of:	
		☐ Protestor	
		☐ Protestee	
	Date	☐	

APPENDIX 7—Protest Form

	Date	Time	Event		Class	Race Number
TO	Organising Club					
FROM	Protesting yacht, sail number and name				Club	
	Represented by	Name			Address	
		Phone				
AGAINST	Protested yacht, sail number and name				Club	
	Has the yacht been informed of the protest?				☐ Yes How, when? ☐ No Why?	
ABOUT	Time and whereabouts of the incident				Protest flag displayed? ☐ Yes When? ☐ No	

DIAGRAM	Wind Direction	Description
		Force of wind Force of current Rule(s) infringed

WITNESSES	Name	Yacht
	Name	Yacht
SIGNATURE	Signature of the representative of the protesting yacht	

APPENDIX 8—International Juries

An organising authority may appoint an international jury from whose decisions there shall be no appeal, in accordance with rules 1.4, Protest Committees, and 1.5, Right of Appeal, provided that the jury remains constituted as stated herein.

1   Constitution

1.1   An international jury shall consist of a chairman, a vice-chairman, and other members sufficient for a total membership of at least five.

1.2   When the membership is reduced below the required minimum by illness or emergency, and no qualified replacements are available, the jury remains properly constituted provided that it consists of at least three members, all from different countries (in Group I - South and West South America and Group N - Central and East South America, two may be from one country).

1.3   When it is considered desirable that some members should not participate in the discussion and decision of a **protest**, and at least three members remain, the jury remains properly constituted. For the purpose of rule 71.2, Interested Parties, members shall not be regarded as "**interested parties**" by reason of their nationality.

1.4   When the jury acts while not properly constituted, its decisions shall be subject to appeal to the national authority.

2   Membership

2.1   The officers and other members of the jury shall be appointed by the organising authority, subject to approval by the national authority when so required in accordance with rule 1.4(d), Protest Committees, from amongst experienced yachtsmen having extensive knowledge of the **rules** and protest committee or jury experience. In addition, a secretary without vote may be appointed.

2.2   The jury shall be separate from and independent of the race committee and shall not include any member of the race committee.

2.3   A majority shall be international judges certified by the IYRU.

2.4   Not more than two members (three when the event is held in Group I - South and West South America or Group N - Central and East South America) shall be from the same country, except that, when there is more than one panel, the requirements for the membership of a jury shall apply to each panel and not to the jury as a whole.

3   Functions

3.1   To determine whether **protests** are valid or invalid.

3.2   To hear and decide **protests** in accordance with the rules of Part VI, Protests, Penalties and Appeals.

3.3 To penalise yachts in accordance with rule 70.1(b), Action by Race or Protest Committee.

3.4 To call hearings in accordance with rule 70.2, Action by Race or Protest Committee.

3.5 To initiate considerations of redress in accordance with rule 70.3, Yacht Materially Prejudiced, and rule 74.2, Consideration of Redress.

3.6 To re-open hearings in accordance with rule 73.6, Re-opening a Hearing.

3.7 When requested, to assist the race committee or the organising authority, particularly on such matters as may directly affect the fairness of the competition.

3.8 Unless otherwise specifically directed by the organising authority:

   (a) to decide questions of eligibility, measurement or ratings of yachts.

   (b) to authorise the substitution of competitors, yachts, sails or equipment.

3.9 When specifically directed by the organising authority:

   (a) to initiate or authorise changes in or additions to the sailing instructions.

   (b) to supervise or direct the race committee in the conduct of the races.

   (c) to deal with such other matters as may be requested.

4 Procedures

4.1 Decisions of the jury shall be made by a simple majority vote, each member having one vote. When there is an equality of votes cast, the chairman of the meeting shall be entitled to an additional vote.

4.2 The jury may be divided into panels of at least five members each, of which a majority shall be international judges certified by the IYRU. When a panel fails to agree on a decision, it may adjourn and refer the case to the full jury.

4.3 When the national authority prescribes that its approval is required for the appointment of an international jury, its approval shall be included in the notice of race or the sailing instructions, or be posted on the official notice board.

APPENDIX 9—Excerpts from the International Regulations for Preventing Collisions at Sea, 1972

At 1200 Zone time, July 15, 1977, the International Regulations for Preventing Collisions at Sea, 1972 came into effect in most waters of the world. Excerpts from these which might affect right of way between yachts *racing* when in effect in accordance with rule 3.2(b)(xxix), Race Continues after Sunset, are as follows:

Part A—General

Rule 3

General Definitions

(a) The word "vessel" includes every description of water craft, including nondisplacement craft and seaplanes, used or capable of being used as a means of transportation on water.

(b) The term "sailing vessel" means any vessel under sail provided that propelling machinery, if fitted, is not being used.

Part B—Steering and Sailing Rules

SECTION I—CONDUCT OF VESSELS IN ANY CONDITION OF VISIBILITY

Rule 4

Application

Rules in this Section apply in any condition of visibility.

Rule 5

Look-out

Every vessel shall at all times maintain a proper look-out by sight and hearing as well as by all available means appropriate in the prevailing circumstances and conditions so as to make a full appraisal of the situation and of the risk of collision.

Rule 6

Safe Speed

Every vessel shall at all times proceed at a safe speed so that she can take proper and effective action to avoid collision and be stopped within a distance appropriate to the prevailing circumstances and conditions.

Rule 7

Risk of Collision

(a) Every vessel shall use all available means appropriate to the prevailing circumstances and conditions to determine if risk of collision exists. If there is any doubt such risk shall be deemed to exist.

Rule 8

Action to avoid Collision

(b) Any action taken to avoid collision shall, if the circumstances of the case admit, be positive, made in ample time and with due regard to the observance of good seamanship.

SECTION II—CONDUCT OF VESSELS IN SIGHT OF ONE ANOTHER

Rule 11

Application

Rules in this Section apply to vessels in sight of one another.

Rule 12

Sailing Vessels

(a) When two sailing vessels are approaching one another, so as to involve risk of collision, one of them shall keep out of the way of the other as follows:

    (i) when each has the wind on a different side, the vessel which has the wind on the port side shall keep out of the way of the other;

    (ii) when both have the wind on the same side, the vessel which is to windward shall keep out of the way of the vessel which is to leeward;

    (iii) if a vessel with the wind on the port side sees a vessel to windward and cannot determine with certainty whether the other vessel has the wind on the port or on the starboard side, she shall keep out of the way of the other.

(b) For the purposes of this Rule the windward side shall be deemed to be the side opposite to that on which the mainsail is carried or, in the case of a square-rigged vessel, the side opposite to that on which the largest fore-and-aft sail is carried.

Rule 13

Overtaking

(a) Notwithstanding anything contained in the Rules of this Section any vessel overtaking any other shall keep out of the way of the vessel being overtaken.

(b) A vessel shall be deemed to be overtaking when coming up with another vessel from a direction more than 22.5 degrees abaft her beam, that is, in such a position with reference to the vessel she is overtaking, that at night she would be able to see only the sternlight of that vessel but neither of her sidelights.

(c) When a vessel is in any doubt as to whether she is overtaking another, she shall assume that this is the case and act accordingly.

(d) Any subsequent alteration of the bearing between the two vessels shall not make the overtaking vessel a crossing vessel within the meaning of these rules or relieve her of the duty of keeping clear of the overtaken vessel until she is finally past and clear.

Rule 16

Action by Give-way Vessel

Every vessel which is directed to keep out of the way of another vessel shall, so far as possible, take early and substantial action to keep well clear.

Rule 17

Action by Stand-on Vessel

(a) (i) Where one of two vessels is to keep out of the way the other shall keep her course and speed.

(ii) The latter vessel may however take action to avoid collision by her manoeuvre alone, as soon as it becomes apparent to her that the vessel required to keep out of the way is not taking appropriate action in compliance with these Rules.

(b) When, from any cause, the vessel required to keep her course and speed finds herself so close that collision cannot be avoided by the action of the give-way vessel alone, she shall take such action as will best aid to avoid collision.

(c) This Rule does not relieve the give-way vessel of her obligation to keep out of the way.

Rule 18

Responsibilities between Vessels

Except where Rule 13 otherwise requires:

(b) A sailing vessel underway shall keep out of the way of:

(ii) a vessel restricted in her ability to manoeuvre.

SECTION III—CONDUCT OF VESSELS IN RESTRICTED VISIBILITY

Rule 19

Conduct of Vessels in Restricted Visibility

(a) This Rule applies to vessels not in sight of one another when navigating in or near an area of restricted visibility.

(b) Every vessel shall proceed at a safe speed adapted to the prevailing circumstances and conditions of restricted visibility. A power-driven vessel shall have her engines ready for immediate manoeuvre.

(c) Every vessel shall have due regard to the prevailing circumstances and conditions of restricted visibility when complying with the Rules of Section I of this Part.

(d) Except where it has been determined that a risk of collision does not exist, every vessel which hears apparently forward of her beam the fog signal of another vessel, or which cannot avoid a close-quarters situation with another vessel forward of her beam, shall reduce her speed to the minimum at which she can be kept on her course. She shall if necessary take all her way off and in any event navigate with extreme caution until danger of collision is over.

Note—

These excerpts are not intended to be complete, but are intended to bring to notice the differences between these rules and those of Part IV of the Yacht Racing Rules. Please note that rules affecting sailing vessels are contained in the rules governing Lights and Shapes, and Sound and Light Signals.

APPENDIX 10—Weighing of Wet Clothing (Racing Rule 61)

To test the weight of clothing and equipment worn by a competitor all items to be weighed shall be taken off and thoroughly soaked in water. Note: Equipment includes items such as trapeze harness, life jacket and heavy jacket.

The manner in which the clothing and equipment is arranged on the rack has a considerable effect on the weight recorded, and it is important that free draining is achieved without the formation of pools of water in the clothing. It is recommended that a rack comprised of "clothes hanger" type bars be used and that provision is made for suspending boots or shoes in an inverted position.

Pockets in clothing that are designed to be self-draining - i.e. those that have drain holes and no provision for closing them - shall be empty during the weighing; however, pockets or equipment designed to hold water as ballast shall be full when weighing takes place. Boots and shoes shall be empty when weighed.

Ordinary clothing becomes saturated within a few seconds but "heavy jackets" of the water absorbent type require longer and should be immersed for not less than two minutes.

On removal from the water the items shall be allowed to drain freely for one minute, at the end of which period the weight shall be recorded.

When the weight recorded exceeds the amount permitted, the measurer may allow the competitor to repeat the test twice by rearranging the clothing and equipment on the rack, re-soaking and re-weighing. When a lesser weight results, that weight shall be taken as the actual weight of clothing and equipment.

Appendix 11—Photographic Evidence

Photographs and video recordings may be accepted as evidence at a hearing and can sometimes be useful. However, there are some limitations and problems, and these should be appreciated by the protest committee.

The following points may be of assistance to protest committees when video evidence is used, but many of them apply also to still photographs.

1   When a video recording is to be replayed to the protest committee by a

party to the protest, he should arrange that the necessary machinery be set up in the hearing room and an operator (preferably the person who made the recording) be available to operate it.

2   The party bringing the video evidence should have seen it before the hearing and have reasons why he believes it will assist the committee.

3   It is usually preferable to view the video after the parties have presented their cases.

4   Allow the recording to be viewed first without comment, then with the comments of the party bringing the evidence, then with those of the other party. Questions may be asked in the normal way by the parties and the committee members.

5   The depth perception of any single-lens camera is very poor; with a telephoto lens it is non-existent. When, for example, the camera's view is at right angles to the courses of two overlapped yachts, it is impossible to assess the distance between them. Conversely, when the camera is directly ahead or astern, it is impossible to see when an overlap begins or even if one exists, unless it is substantial. Keep these limitations firmly in mind.

6   Use the first viewing of the tape to become oriented to the scene. Where was the camera in relation to the yachts? What was the angle between them? Was the camera's platform moving? If so, in what direction and how fast? Is the angle changing as the yachts approach the critical point? (Beware of a radical change caused by fast panning of the camera.) Did the camera have an unrestricted view throughout? If not, how much does that diminish the value of the evidence? Full orientation may require several viewings; take the time necessary.

7   Since it takes only about 30 seconds to run and re-wind a typical incident, view it as many times as needed to extract all the information it can give. Also, be sure that the other party has an equal opportunity to point out what he believes it shows and does not show.

8   Hold the equipment in place until the end of the hearing. It is often desirable, during deliberation, to be able to review the tape to settle questions as to just what fact or facts it establishes. Also, one of the members may have noticed something that the others did not.

9   Do not expect too much from the videotape. Only occasionally, from a fortuitous camera angle, will it establish clearly the central fact of an incident. Yet, if it does no more than settle one disputed point, that will help in reaching a correct decision.

APPENDIX 12—Sailing Instructions Guide

This guide provides a set of checked and tested instructions that may be used verbatim for any regatta that will be sailed on a single course. Thus they will be particularly useful for most world, continental, national and other principal events. Also, when a regatta will use more than one course, the sailing instruction regarding courses can be altered appropriately; and most, if not all, other instructions will be applicable as they stand.

Some instructions are required or strongly recommended, while others are optional. Those that are required or recommended are shown with an asterisk (*).

The principles on which all sailing instructions should be based are as follows:

1   They should include only two types of statement: the intentions of the race committee and the obligations of competitors.

2   They should be concerned only with racing. Other information should be communicated through other means. For example: measurement regulations, requirements concerning registration of competitors or yachts, assignment of moorings, liability insurance, etc. should be in different documents.

3   They should not alter the racing rules, unless it is clearly desirable.

4   They should not repeat or restate any of the racing rules.

5   They should not repeat themselves.

6   The order of the instructions should reflect the chronological order in which the competitor will use them.

7   When possible, words or phrases used in the racing rules should be used in writing sailing instructions.

To use the guide in the preparation of sailing instructions, first delete all optional instructions that will not be needed. Then, following the instructions in the left margin, fill in the required information and select the alternatives desired. Finally, re-number all instructions in sequential order.

NOTE: The notes in this column contain guidance for preparing sailing instructions. Do not include them in the completed draft.

Insert: The full name of the regatta. The inclusive dates from measurement or the practice race until the final race. The name of the organising authority. The city and the country.

_____

_____

_____

_____

Sailing Instructions

*1.   **Rules**

Insert the full names of the national authority when applicable, and the class(es).
Insert the appropriate category in accordance with Appendix 14.

The regatta will be governed by the International Yacht Racing Rules, the prescriptions of the ● , the rules of the ● class(es), (except as any of these are altered by these sailing instructions) and by these sailing instructions. The regatta is classified as a Category ● event.

*2   **Entries**

Eligible yachts may be entered by completing registration with the organising authority.

·3   Notices to Competitors

Insert the specific location(s).

Notices to competitors will be posted on the official notice board(s) located ● .

·4   Changes in Sailing Instructions

Insert the times.

Any change in the sailing instructions will be posted before ● on the day it will take effect, except that any change in the schedule of races will be posted by ● on the day before it will take effect.

5   Signals Made Ashore

Insert the specific location.

5.1   Signals made ashore will be displayed at ● .

Insert the sound signal and time.

5.2   Code flag "AP", Answering Pendant, with two ● , (one ● when lowered) means "The race is postponed. The warning signal will be made not less than ● minutes after "AP" is lowered".

Insert the sound signal.

5.3   Code flag "B" at "the dip" with one ● means "Protest time has begun". When fully hoisted it means "There are less than 30 minutes remaining before protest time ends". When lowered it means "Protest time has ended".

·6   Schedule of Races

Insert the days, dates and times.

Races are scheduled as follows:

Race   Day and Date   Time of Warning Signal

7   Class Flags

Insert the class names and descriptions of flags. Use only for a multi-class regatta.

Class flags will be:

Class   Flag

8   Racing Area

A section of a chart or other suitable map should be copied and marked for this purpose.

The racing area will be as shown in illustration "A", attached.

9   The Course

Insert the distances. Delete the last sentence when not applicable.

·9.1   The diagram below shows the course, including the approximate angles between legs, the order in which marks are to be rounded or passed, and the side on which each mark is to be left. Mark 1 will be approximately ● nautical miles from Mark 3. The first and last legs will be approximately ● longer than the distance from Mark 3 to Mark 1.

Insert course diagram(s) here. A method of illustrating a course is shown in Appendix A, Illustrating the Course. When there are navigational marks that are to be observed, they should be shown on the course chart.

9.2 The approximate compass bearing from the starting line to Mark 1 will be displayed from the race committee signal boat.

9.3 Courses will not be shortened.

*10 Marks

Insert the description of the marks and the instruction number.

Marks 1, 2 and 3 will be ● . New marks, when used in accordance with instruction ● , Change of Course after the Start, will be ● . The starting and finishing marks will be ● .

11 The Start

Use the last part of the sentence for a multi-class regatta. Insert the number of minutes.

*11.1 Races will be started in accordance with racing rule 4.4(a) System 1, with classes starting at ● minute intervals in the order ● .

(OR)

*11.1 Races will be started in accordance with racing rule 4.4(a) System 2, with classes starting at ● minute intervals in the order ● .

*11.2 The starting line will be between a staff displaying an orange flag or shape on the race committee boat at the starboard end and Mark 3 at the port end.

(OR)

*11.2 The starting line will be between a staff displaying an orange flag or shape on the race committee boat at the starboard end and the port end starting mark.

(OR)

Delete the last sentence when signals will be made from the starboard end race committee boat.

*11.2 The starting line will be between staffs displaying orange flags or shapes on two race committee boats. Signals will be made from a race committee signal boat stationed to windward of the line.

(OR)

*11.2 (a) The starting line will between staffs displaying orange flags on Starting Marks A and B and between staffs displaying orange flags on Starting Marks B and C as shown below. Mark B may not be on a straight line between Mark A and Mark C.

Mark A ●   ●   ● Mark C
Mark B

(b) For the purpose of racing rules 51.1(b) and 51.1(c), the extensions of the starting line are the extensions beyond Mark A and Mark C.

(c) When a yacht both touches Mark B and infringes racing rule 51.1(c), she may exonerate herself by completing one rounding of either Mark A or Mark C.

Use only for a multi-class regatta. Insert "warning" when classes start at ten-minute intervals, "preparatory" when they start at five-minute intervals.

11.3 Yachts whose ● signal has not been made shall keep clear of the starting area and of all yachts whose ● signal has been made.

Insert the number of minutes.

11.4 A yacht shall not start later than ● minutes after her starting signal.

12 Recalls

Insert "in accordance with racing rule 8.1" or describe any special procedure.

*12.1 Individual recalls will be signalled ●

Use only when a new warning signal is desired after a general recall.

12.2 When a general recall has been signalled, a new warning signal will be made one minute after the lowering of Code flag "First Substitute".

Use only for a multi-class regatta.

12.3 When a general recall has been signalled, the start(s) for the succeeding class(es) will be postponed accordingly.

13 Mark Boats

Insert the description of the flag or shape.

Mark boats will be stationed beyond each mark. At the finish, the mark boat will be stationed beyond the finishing line. When on station only, each mark boat will display a ● . Failure of a mark boat to be on station or to display her signal will not be grounds for redress.

14 Change of Course after the Start

14.1 When changing the course after the start, the race committee will lay a new mark and will lift the original mark as soon as practicable. Any mark to be rounded after rounding the new mark may be relocated to maintain the original course configuration.

Insert the sound signal.

14.2 A change of course will be signalled near the mark beginning the leg being changed by a race committee boat that will display Code flag "C" and the approximate compass bearing to the new mark and sound a ● periodically. The change will be signalled before the leading yacht has begun the leg, although the new mark may not yet be in position.

14.3 When in a subsequent change of course a new mark is replaced, it will be replaced with an original mark.

*15 The Finish

The finishing line will be between a staff displaying an orange flag or shape on a race committee boat and Mark 1 at the port end.

(OR)

The finishing line will be between a staff displaying an orange flag or shape on a race committee boat and the port end finishing mark.

(OR)

The finishing line will be between staffs displaying orange flags or shapes on two race committee boats.

*16 Time Limit

Insert the time(s) and class(es). Adjust for a single class regatta or for a single time limit for all classes.

The time limit will be ● for the ● class and ● for the ● class. Yachts finishing more than ● minutes after the first yacht finishes or after the time limit, whichever is later, will be scored "Did not finish".

17 Protests

Insert the location and time.

17.1 Protests shall be written on forms available at ● and lodged there within ● after the time of the last yacht's finish.

(OR)

Insert the location and time.

17.1 Protests shall be written on forms available at ● and lodged there within Protest Time which will begin ● and end ● later.

Substitute "race committee" or "protest committee" for "jury" when there is no jury. See above. Insert the time.

17.2 The jury will hear protests in approximately the order of receipt as soon as possible.

(OR)

17.2 The jury will hear protests in approximately the order of receipt beginning at ●

17.3 Protest notices will be posted within 30 minutes of the protest time limit to inform competitors where and when there is a hearing in which they are parties to a protest or named as witnesses.

Use only when the requirements of rule 1.5 are met.

17.4 Decisions of the jury will be final in accordance with racing rule 1.5.

*18 **Scoring**

The Olympic Scoring System, Appendix 5.1 of the racing rules, will apply.

(OR)

Use when the Olympic Scoring System is desired but the number of scheduled races is other than seven. Insert the number of races. See Appendix 5.1 for other possible alterations.

The Olympic Scoring System, Appendix 5.1 of the racing rules, will apply, except that ● races are scheduled, of which ● races shall be completed to constitute a series.

(OR)

See Appendix 5.2 for possible alterations.

The Low-Point Scoring System, Appendix 5.2 of the racing rules, will apply.

(OR)

State the scoring system to apply by reference to the class rules or other document containing the complete scoring system.

_____

_____

_____

19 **Alternative Penalties**

The 720° Turns penalty, Appendix 3.1 of the racing rules, will apply.

(OR)

The Percentage penalty, Appendix 3.2 of the racing rules, will apply.

20 **Support Boats**

Insert the dates or times.

Team leaders, coaches and other support personnel shall not go afloat in the racing area between ● inclusive except in boats provided by the organising authority. The penalty for failing to comply with this requirement may be the disqualification of all yachts associated with the infringing support personnel.

21 **Haul-out Restrictions**

When this applies to some classes only, insert the name(s) of the class(es) between "all" and "yachts". Insert the time. Substitute "race committee" or "protest committee" for "jury" when there is no jury. Use (b) only when there is a scheduled reserve day.

All yachts shall be afloat before ● on the day preceding the first scheduled race and shall not be hauled out during the regatta except:

(a) with and according to the terms of prior written permission of the jury; or

(b) after the race preceding a reserve day. In which case they shall again be afloat before ● on the day preceding the next race.

22 Plastic Pools and Diving Equipment

Insert the class(es) and time.

Underwater breathing apparatus, plastic pools or their equivalent shall not be used around ● class yachts after ● on the day preceding the first scheduled race.

23 Radio Communication

A yacht shall neither make radio transmissions while racing nor receive special radio communications not available to all yachts.

24 Prizes

Alter as required. When perpetual trophies are to be awarded, refer to them by their complete names.

Prizes will be awarded to each member of the crews placing first, second and third in the regatta.

Appendix A—Illustrating the Course

Shown here is a recommended method for illustrating a course. Any course can be similarly shown, using the same details. When there is more than one course, prepare separate diagrams for each and state how each course will be signalled.

This course is a typical "Olympic" course: triangle, windward, leeward, windward, on a 45°-90°-45° triangle. In this example the starting and finishing lines are separate and are between two race committee boats. The third sentence of instruction 9.1 and the third versions of instructions 11.2 and 15 would be used.

Start-1-2-3-1-3-Finish
Marks to be rounded to port

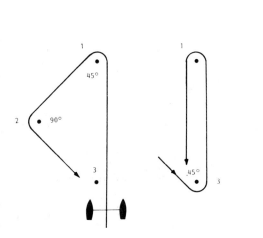

In the next example the course is the same except that the starting and finishing lines are between a race committee boat and Marks 3 and 1 respectively. The third sentence of instruction 9.1 would be deleted and the first versions of instructions 11.2 and 15 would be used.

Start-1-2-3-1-3-Finish
Marks to be rounded to port.

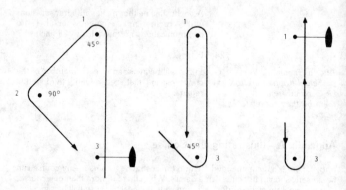

Appendix B—Yachts provided by the Organising Authority

The following sailing instruction should be used when all yachts will be provided by the organising authority.

The instruction can be added to or altered, or portions deleted to suit the situation. When used, it should be inserted following instruction 5, Signals Made Ashore.

X   **Yachts**

X.1   Yachts will be provided for all competitors, who shall not modify them or cause them to be modified in any way except that:

(a) a compass may be tied or taped to the hull or spars;

(b) wind indicators, including yarn or thread, may be tied or taped anywhere on the yacht;

(c) hulls, centreboards and rudders may be cleaned only with water;

(d) adhesive tape may be used anywhere above the water line; and

(e) all fittings or equipment designed to be adjusted may be adjusted, provided that the class rules are observed.

X.2 All equipment provided with the yacht for sailing purposes shall be carried while afloat.

X.3 The penalty for infringement of the above instructions will be disqualification from all races sailed in contravention of the instruction.

Substitute "race committee" or "protest committee" for "jury" when there is no jury.

X.4 Competitors shall report any damage or loss of equipment, however slight, to the organising authority's representative immediately after securing the yacht ashore. The penalty for infringement of this instruction, unless the jury is satisfied that the competitor made a determined effort to comply, will be disqualification from the race most recently sailed.

Use when the regatta is not restricted to class members.

X.5 Class rules requiring competitors to be members of the class association will not apply.

Appendix C—Gate Start

When this instruction is used, instruction 9, The Course, should show the starting area on the diagram, indicating the Port Limit Mark. This instruction replaces instruction 11, The Start. Instruction 12.1 will not be used.

11 Gate Start

11.1 Starting marks will be:

Describe the mark.

(a) The Port Limit Mark, a ● on the starboard side of the race committee boat.

(b) The Pathfinder.

(c) The Gate Launch, displaying Code flag "G".

(d) The Guard Boat, displaying Code flag "U".

Insert the system to be used. Insert the number of minutes.

11.2 The signals for starting will be in accordance with racing rule 4.4(a) System ● displayed from the race committee boat, which will also display Code flag "G", signifying a gate start. At or before the warning signal, numeral pendant ● will be displayed indicating the time in minutes between the starting signal and the time at which the Gate Launch will stop at the starboard end of the starting line.

11.3 The Pathfinder for the first race sailed will be appointed by the race committee. The Pathfinder for subsequent races will be the yacht that finished tenth in the preceding race. When this yacht is unable to race or has acted as Pathfinder previously, the Pathfinder will be appointed by the race committee and will normally be the yacht that finished eleventh in the preceding race. The national letters and sail number of the Pathfinder will be posted on the official notice board each day. Prior to the preparatory signal, the Pathfinder shall report to the Gate Launch, which will be near the Port Limit Mark.

11.4 After the preparatory signal, yachts shall not sail on the windward side of an imaginary line which would be the course of a yacht sailing from the Port Limit Mark on a close-hauled port tack.

11.5 Approximately ten seconds prior to the starting signal:

(a) the Pathfinder will begin a close-hauled port tack from the Port Limit Mark,

(b) the Gate Launch will keep station close astern of the Pathfinder, and

(c) the Guard Boat may escort the Pathfinder on her starboard side.

11.6 The starting line (except for the Pathfinder) will be between the Port Limit Mark and the centre of the stern of the Gate Launch.

11.7 All yachts (except for the Pathfinder) shall start on starboard tack after the starting signal. A yacht starting prematurely shall retire from the race. Racing rule 8.1, Individual Recall, shall not apply.

11.8 The Pathfinder shall sail her close-hauled course until she is released by hail from the Gate Launch, after which she may continue on port tack or tack, as she wishes.

11.9 After the release of the Pathfinder, the Gate Launch will continue her course and speed until the gate has been opened for the period signalled in instruction 11.2. She will then stop, make a long sound signal, drift for one minute, and finally signal the close of the gate by lowering Code flag "G" with a short sound signal. Thereafter, no yacht shall start.

11.10 Before *starting*, a yacht shall not interfere with the Pathfinder. Any yacht that interferes with, or passes between, or attempts to pass between the Pathfinder, the Gate Launch or the Guard Boat, or that causes another yacht to interfere in any of these ways, or that is on the port side of the Gate Launch as she opens the gate, shall retire from that race and shall be ineligible for any re-starts of that race, unless the infringing yacht can satisfy the race committee that her actions were caused either by another yacht not having right of way, or by some other unavoidable circumstance. Racing rule 8.2(b) shall not apply.

APPENDIX 13 — Guide for Principal Events

REGATTA ORGANISATION: A PLANNING CHECKLIST

Addressed to regatta chairmen, race officers, sub-committee chairmen, and others involved in the planning and conduct of a principal national or international championship, this checklist is a list of functions usually required or desirable for an important regatta. A single class event is assumed, although the checklist can be adapted to meet different needs.

The checklist is simply a list of topics, grouped roughly in chronological order, or into broad functional areas. The regatta's general chairman with his sub-committee chairmen should draw up a regatta plan by asking themselves, for each topic, the following: what is to be accomplished?, what procedures will be followed?, what are requirements for space or facilities, personnel, and money?, and by what date must it be done?.

The checklist does not discuss race management, the single most important element in a successful regatta. The second part of this appendix, "Guide for Race Officers", offers advice about race management for world, continental, national, and other principal events. More general race management guides are available from several national authorities and class associations.

1. Establish basic details, such as dates, location, number of races, racing area, and extent of measurement.

2. Establish communication with the class association (international and national), the national authority, local government authorities (including police and navy or coast guard), other organisations that use the sailing waters (e.g., water ski or fishing clubs), and city or regional visitors' information office.

3. Appoint the race officer and the chairman of the jury. Establish the relationship between the race committee and jury (note racing rules 1.4 and 1.5; also Appendix 8).

4. Appoint chairmen of sub-committees and other key personnel, for: measurement, registration and regatta office, publicity and press relations, housing assistance, boat shipping assistance, interpreters, launching and mooring, social events, scoring, budget control, trophies, opening and closing ceremonies, buildings and grounds maintenance, jury secretary, and special hospitality. The general chairman is the head of the regatta organisation. For each area of responsibility determine the number of people required and any special qualifications. (Example: the jury should include at least one member familiar with the class.)

5. Establish the budget, including income from entry fees, sponsorship support (if any), governmental or private grants, programme advertising revenue, sales of food and drink, and subsidy from the national authority, class

association or host club. Include expense estimates for such items as printing, fuel, equipment rental, jury travel and housing, catering service, computer and copy machine rental, postage and telephone, trophies, souvenirs or participants' awards, extra janitorial or other staff, security service, measurement and jig materials, tent rental, and food and drink supplies. Include in the budget goods or services provided without charge, on both the income and the expense lists.

6. Publish and distribute advance information including the notice of race (see racing rule 2). Include basic details (see 1, above); organising authority's address, telex and telephone; eligibility requirements; entry fee (and what it includes); schedule for measurement and racing; sailing area, including distance from the regatta site; current, water depth, and any weed growth; housing availability, including hotel prices and distance from the club, camping, guest houses, and university dormitories; meal arrangements and facilities; general visitors' information and map of city or area; boat shipping and travel advice; social events; climate and weather data; postal address for participants; customs information; launching and mooring arrangements; maximum number of sails and spars to be measured; yacht charter availability; regulations affecting coach or team boats; haul-out restrictions; whether advertising on yachts or clothing is permitted (see racing rule 26 and Appendix 14); and any special dress requirements. Distribute this information to national authorities; national class associations; class newsletter editors; yachting magazines; local newspapers; TV and radio stations; and class sailmakers, boat builders and distributors. Enter the event on the IYRU or the national authority's fixture list.

7. Arrange for all equipment and supplies, including race committee boats, marks, and radios, by borrowing, rental or purchase. Negotiate written contracts when appropriate. Fill remaining personnel assignments. All sub-committees should now make recommendations about their procedures with a complete list of responsibilities; regular meetings should be held by the general chairman with all key personnel. Examples of equipment needs are: marine radios, spectator and press boats, cranes and scales for weighing yachts and wet clothing, typewriters, copiers, notice boards, flagpoles, hand-bearing compasses, computer terminal, measurement jigs, competitors' mailboxes, jury room equipment, safe for prizes or money, public address system, and first aid supplies.

8. Arrange for special space or facilities not normally available at the regatta site, such as: car and trailer parking, extra toilets, sail and yacht measurement space, extra public telephones, press office, sail-drying area, regatta office, fresh water for boat washing, food and drink sales area, and repair area.

9. Arrange for services and information for competitors and visitors, such as: daily weather information; information about local chandlers, sailmakers, and boat builders; currency exchange or banks; medical and dental emergency resources; and travel agencies and airlines. Post signs before the event.

10. Prepare the sailing instructions, drafted by the race officer conferring with the general chairman, class association president or secretary, and jury chairman. Refer to racing rule 3, the Appendix 12 Sailing Instructions Guide, and class rules governing the conduct of class championships.

11. Prepare the regatta programme; to include all information of interest to competitors, other visitors, regatta workers, and press representatives. Consider each item listed above, and additionally: welcome messages from dignitaries; recommended restaurants and approximate prices; names of

jury members, race committee and other important regatta workers; brief history of the class or the event, and of the club; notable local civic attractions; schedule of all events; and past winners of the championship. Do not include the sailing instructions, which should be published separately.

12. Final steps, before racing begins, include publication of the entry list, including all competitors' names; confirming that all eligibility and entry requirements, including measurement, have been completed; issuance of competitor "packets", including badges, tickets, gifts, invitations, car or trailer stickers, and maps; jury organisational meeting; final meeting of sub-committee chairmen; competitors' meeting (if any); press briefing.

13. During the regatta the general chairman should confer daily with key sub-committee chairmen, early enough to allow any changes of procedure or announcements. Conferring with a class spokesman is also advisable. He should also satisfy himself that all duties are being performed as planned.

14. At the close of the series and afterwards, provide for: assistance to competitors in hauling and loading their yachts; perpetual trophies being boxed, and signed for by their winners; copies of final results for all competitors, officials, class association and press; return of all borrowed and rented equipment; payment of bills, collection of receipts, and final budget report; letters of thanks; reports with recommendations from the race officer, jury chairman and other key personnel; and general chairman's recommendations to the class association and next host club.

There is one other essential element, not contained anywhere in the above list, that determines in large measure how the regatta will be judged by its participants. This is the degree to which visitors are made to feel welcome by regatta workers, club members, officials, local merchants, and others in the community. This job cannot be assigned to a committee or included in the budget. Yet it can be discussed in the planning process and should be a consideration in making decisions. It is everyone's job.

GUIDE FOR RACE OFFICERS

This guide is intended for the race officer who has had previous race committee experience and is therefore familiar with basic race management procedures. It contains suggestions and advice for the conduct of the racing at any principal event, when unusual problems may be caused by the importance of the event or size of fleet, and when the expectations of competitors and other regatta participants require race committee work of the highest standard.

BASIC GOAL AND OBJECTIVES

The goal of the race committee for a principal event is to provide the best possible racing, as measured by accepted standards of yacht racing in general, and by the requirements of the class or other body that sets the conditions of the event. Accordingly, certain objectives become clear:

1. The racing rules that affect the conduct of the racing (Part II in particular) should be closely adhered to, and altered only when the need is clear.

2. Class rules that govern the event (e.g., those that specify the number of races, course configuration and course length), and any other conditions that may be applicable, should be recognised and applied.

3.   The quality of the race committee and its equipment should be as high as possible.

These objectives can be met through careful planning, preparation, and practice before the event.

PLANNING—FIRST STEPS

The race officer should help to draft the notice of race, expressing his views on the relevant items listed in racing rule 2. He should obtain a current copy of the class rules, for reference to requirements for the conduct of class events, and may also wish to establish early contact with a class officer who, both before and during the regatta, can be helpful with information and suggestions. The race officer will also want to appoint the key members of his race committee.

SAILING INSTRUCTIONS

The race officer should be the principal draftsman of the sailing instructions, using Appendix 12, Sailing Instructions Guide, and any class rules governing the conduct of the event. He should seek the views of the class liaison person, the chairman of the jury or protest committee, and the general chairman, before the final draft is agreed.

COMMITTEE PERSONNEL

Race committee members should be experienced sailors as well as having had race committee experience, and should be physically capable of working long hours on the water in occasionally trying conditions. Within reason, the smaller the committee, the better - small boats can then be used (see "Equipment"), communication can be simplified, and action will occur with a minimum of time loss. A feeling of accomplishing tasks with good team work and a minimum of fuss is another by-product.

EQUIPMENT

Race committee boats should be small, fast, and designed for local waters. Marks should be large, inflatable, and towable, coloured high-visibility orange when possible, with dependable ground tackle. Radios should be hand-held, but with one larger unit capable of reaching regatta headquarters on shore. Flags or shapes should be very large. Sound signals are best made with shotguns or small cannons and with highly audible horns or athletic referee whistles. Ground tackle for race committee boats and marks should be thoroughly tested in advance.

Each race committee boat should have a checklist of all equipment that should be on board before departure for the racing area; the list should be checked before each race.

LAYING MARKS

Laying the windward and gybe marks should be delayed until shortly before the start. One procedure is to have both marks laid by a single, fast boat that proceeds upwind first, positioning the windward mark by use of a hand-held compass sighting back toward the starting line, then proceeding to lay the gybe mark by taking compass bearings on both the windward mark and the mark at the starting area.

THE START

Starting lines should be either between two race committee boats, or between a race committee boat and a mark with a race committee boat stationed beyond it. In either case, when a race committee boat marks an end of the line, the line itself should be identified by a flag or shape, preferably coloured high-visibility orange. Anchor lines should be weighted a few metres below the surface, to prevent yachts from fouling them, and should be capable of rapid adjustment, to facilitate changing the line. The line should be carefully and quickly adjusted to be perpendicular to the wind direction, unless current, wind or other factors make a bias necessary to spread the yachts evenly along the line. Length should be adequate, but not excessive. Starts should not be delayed unless conditions are unsuitable.

For fleets of 40 or more yachts, a two part starting line should be considered, with an additional race committee boat centred between the other marks. Recommended sailing instructions for this system are included in Appendix 12, Sailing Instructions Guide.

Such a system, in combination with a well-laid line, is a proven method of reducing the number of unidentified premature starters. With any system, race committee members should be stationed at each end of the line to identify premature starters.

STARTING PROBLEMS AND SOLUTIONS

The problem of premature starters and general recalls has been common at principal events that have attracted a large number of entries. The solution to this problem is actually several solutions used together. The race committee must be organised so that it can adjust the angle of the starting line quickly, moving both ends of the line when necessary, right up to the time of the preparatory signal. Good radio contact between all boats is essential. Individual recall signals should be made as soon as possible. Taken together, all of these details will show the committee's intention to provide a good start and to detect any premature starters.

For fleets of more than 30 yachts, the use of racing rule 51.1(c) for all starts is desirable. Sailing instructions providing for disqualification of yachts that are above the line before the start, or within a specified time period before the start, are rarely necessary and are not recommended unless all other methods fail.

Other starting problems include strong up-wind currents in light airs; deep water, making anchoring difficult; limited visibility; light and extremely variable winds; etc. Each of them can be trying to officials and sailors alike; the experienced race officer will select his equipment with care (the anchoring problem), will know when postponement should be considered (problems of unstable wind, or visibility), and in certain circumstances should not be averse to hailing yachts (using Code flag "L") before the start about hazards threatening the start (the current problem). Generally the well-prepared race committee, directed by a thoughtful level-headed race officer, will find solutions when required.

ABANDONMENT AFTER THE START

Increasingly, competitors at principal championships prefer to have a race in progress stopped and re-started when, for example, a major and unpredictable wind shift helps some yachts and hurts others to the extent that the race is not considered a satisfactory test of skill. Any provision permitting abandonment and re-sail of a race in such circumstances should be discussed in advance with class representatives, and should be included in the sailing instructions as a clarification of racing rule 5.4(c).

PRESERVATION OF COURSE CONFIGURATION

After the start the race committee should continually watch for any changes of wind direction that will threaten the course configuration, and be prepared to take corrective action by relocating one or more marks. This is best done by laying a new mark with different visual characteristics, then removing the old mark. The Sailing Instructions Guide provides wording that describes the race committee's signalling procedure and other details of the sequence of events for use when marks will be changed.

It is more important to change some legs of the course than others, because a change of wind direction has greater effect on the quality of the leg. For example: the dead run, which yachts sail best by gybing from one tack to the other in response to changes in wind direction or strength, can be reduced to a one-tack reaching leg, offering no strategic or tactical challenges, when the wind direction changes only 15 to 20 degrees. Corrective action will require relocation of the leeward mark, signalling the change at the windward mark as the fleet rounds it. Windward legs are also damaged by major wind shifts, and most race committees are sensitive to this. Reaching legs are least subject to damage, and usually need not be changed except as a consequence of changing one of the other legs.

Maintaining the original, intended course configuration is perhaps the committee's most important task after the start.

RESCUE, SPECTATOR CONTROL AND JURY BOATS

Boats for these purposes should be different from the race committee boats, but the race officer should be in communication with them, with authority to direct spectator control boats. All three types of boat will be able to provide assistance on occasion, and should be asked to defer to the race officer's wishes, except in unusual circumstances.

PREPARATION: THE PRACTICE RACE AND BEFORE

When the race officer will be working at a club or other location not familiar to him, and with equipment and people with whom he has not worked regularly, he should make a point of attending an earlier event, and either closely observe or participate in its race management. He will then be in a position to recommend equipment changes, plan his own procedures, and generally familiarise himself with local conditions.

When a race officer and his committee have worked together at the regatta site before, the practice race will be the time to test any new equipment or procedures, and then make changes accordingly. A practice race is desirable, both for the benefit of competitors who may not have raced there before, but also (and perhaps primarily) for the benefit of the race management team.

MEETING OF COMPETITORS

A meeting of all competitors (not only helmsmen) before the practice race serves to convey the race committee's intention to offer the best possible racing and to learn of any unforeseen problems or questions that might require solutions. However, the meeting should not be used to read, discuss or answer questions about the sailing instructions. Such questions should be accepted in written form only, the questions and their answers to be posted on the official notice board. Competitors should be informed of this procedure at the time they complete entry formalities.

IMPORTANT LIAISONS

Before and during the event, the race officer should establish good relationships with the general chairman of the event, to whom he or she is directly accountable; a representative of the class association(s), who will be an invaluable source of information about class requirements and general preferences (e.g., concerning maximum or minimum wind velocities in which races should be started); the chairman of the jury, with whom daily procedures for communication after the race should be established; and the chief scorer, for the same reason. Brief, daily meetings with most of these officials will be productive.

RECORDS

The race committee should keep records in writing and on tape recorders for later reference by the committee, the jury, or the scorers. Such records should include sail numbers of yachts that arrive at the starting area, those that start prematurely or in violation of rule 51.1(c), any yachts involved in apparent rule infringements, the order of finish, and any protest flags observed or reports of protest intentions received at the finish. When possible, the order of roundings at all marks should be taken, but only when boats and people are available for this secondary task.

PRESSURES ON THE RACE OFFICER

Other than the conduct of the racing itself, the race officer may be subject to pressures that may hinder the working of the race committee. He should insist that only race committee members will be aboard race committee boats. Jury members should be aboard separate jury boats. Class officers, other "VIP's", press people, and others wishing to go afloat should be accommodated by the general regatta organisation, when possible, and this should not affect the race committee in any way. Finally, social events should be adjusted to accommodate the racing, when this becomes necessary for the completion of the race schedule.

FURTHER READING

Several national authorities make available detailed manuals or guides on race management. Those in English include the Royal Yachting Association's *Race Management Handbook* and the United States Yacht Racing Union's *Race Management Handbook*. Other manuals have been published by other national authorities in several languages. Class associations also have published guides containing race management procedures, usually relevant for the championships of the class.

APPENDIX 14—Event Classification and Advertising

(No changes are contemplated before 1993. However, the Permanent Committee may approve changes in the interim.)

1   General

1.1   This appendix shall apply when *racing* and, in addition, unless otherwise prescribed in the notice of race, from 0700 on the first race day of a regatta or series until the expiry of the time limit for lodging protests following the last race of the regatta or series.

1.2   Events shall be classified as Category A, B or C in accordance with paragraphs 2, 3 and 4 of this appendix. Unless otherwise prescribed in the notice of race and the sailing instructions, an event shall be classified as Category A.

1.3   The notice of race and the sailing instructions for any category of event may prescribe more restrictive criteria than are otherwise required for that category.

1.4   The IYRU, a national authority, the Offshore Racing Council (ORC) or a class association may develop rules for sanctioning events within its jurisdiction in any or all categories, as well as for giving consent for individual advertisements. Fees may be required.

1.5   Advertised products shall comply with moral and ethical standards.

1.6   In world and continental events, unless so prescribed by the class rules, a competitor shall not be required or induced to display advertising on a yacht, clothing or equipment.

1.7   Governmental requirements affecting yachts shall override this appendix only to the extent that they are inconsistent with it.

1.8   The following advertising is permitted at all times:

(a)   one sailmaker's mark (which may include the name or mark of the manufacturer of the sail cloth and pattern or model description of the sail) may be displayed on each side of any sail. The whole of such a mark shall be placed not more than 15% of the length of the foot of the sail or 300 mm from its tack, whichever is the greater. This latter limitation shall not apply to the position of marks on spinnakers.

(b)   one builder's mark (which may include the name or mark of the designer) may be placed on the hull, and one maker's mark may be displayed on spars and equipment.

(c)   such marks (or plates) shall fit within a square not exceeding 150 mm × 150 mm.

(d)   one maker's mark may be displayed on each item of clothing and equipment worn by the crew, provided that the mark fits within a square not exceeding 100 mm × 100 mm.

(e)   the yacht's type may be displayed once on each side of the hull, provided that the lettering shall not exceed 1% in height and 5% in length of the overall length of the yacht, but not exceeding a maximum height of 100 mm and a maximum length of 700 mm.

(f)   a sailboard's type may be displayed on the hull in two places. The lettering shall not exceed 200 mm in height.

1.9   After obtaining the approval, when relevant, of the national authority, ORC and/or class association, the organising authority of a sponsored event may permit or require advertising by the sponsor on yachts and sailboards only within the following limitations:

(a)   On yachts: the display of a flag and/or the application to the hulls of a decal or sticker, neither of which shall be larger than 45 cm × 60 cm.

(b)   On sailboards: the display of not more than two stickers, one on each side of the sail, each of which shall fit within a rectangle of 2,500 cm², none of the sides of which shall exceed 80 cm in length. The notice of race shall state whether one or both sides of the sail are to be used. When both sides are used, the stickers shall be placed back to back. The stickers shall be placed above the wishbone and at least partly in the lower half of the sail.

(c) Such permission or requirement shall be prescribed in the notice of race.

1.10 When a **protest committee** after finding the facts decides that a yacht or her crew has infringed this appendix, rule 74.4, Penalties and Exoneration, shall not apply, and the **protest committee** shall:

(a) warn the infringing yacht that a further infringement will result in action under rule 70.2, Action by Race or Protest Committee, or

(b) disqualify the yacht, or

(c) when the infringement occurs when the yacht is not *racing,* disqualify the yacht from the race most recently *sailed* or from the next race *sailed* after the infringement, or

(d) when it decides that there was a gross breach of the appendix, disqualify the yacht from more than one race or from the whole series.

2   Category A

Except as permitted in accordance with paragraphs 1.8 and 1.9, a yacht competing in a Category A event shall not display advertising on her hull, spars, sails and equipment and, while aboard the yacht, on the clothing and equipment worn by the crew.

3   Category B

In addition to the advertising permitted by paragraphs 1.8 and 1.9, a yacht competing in a Category B event may display advertising only in accordance with paragraphs 3.1 to 3.4, and a sailboard in accordance with paragraph 3.5.

3.1 ADVERTISING ON YACHTS—GENERAL

(a) A yacht shall not display the advertisements of more than two organisations at one time.

(b) Each advertisement shall consist of one or two of the following:

(i) the name of the organisation;

(ii) one brand or product name;

(iii) one logo.

3.2 ADVERTISING ON HULLS

(a) The forward 25% of the length overall of the hull, including the deck, shall be clear of any individual advertising. This area is reserved for the requirements of the IYRU, national authorities, the ORC or class associations.

(b) 50% of the remaining 75% of the length overall of the hull may be used for individual advertising.

3.3 ADVERTISING ON SAILS

(a) Advertising on spinnakers is without restriction, except as provided in paragraph 3.3(c).

(b) On other sails, only one advertisement may be carried at any one time, and it may be on both sides of one sail. It shall be placed below an imaginary line between the mid-points of the luff and leech of the sail, and have a width of not more than two-thirds of the length of the foot of the sail and a height of not more than one-third of that width.

(c) Advertisements on all sails shall be clearly separated from, and below, the sail numbers.

3.4 ADVERTISING ON SPARS

(a) One-third of the main mast may be used.

(b) Two-thirds of the main boom may be used.

(c) Advertising on the mast or boom shall be limited to the name, or logo of one of the organisations.

3.5 ADVERTISING ON SAILBOARDS

(a) The upper half of the sail above the wishbone may carry only the logo of a sailboard manufacturer.

(b) The tack corner on each side of the sail may carry one label or logo either of a sailboard manufacturer or a sailmaker.

(c) The lower half of the sail above the wishbone may carry only the logo of a sailmaker.

(d) The space below the wishbone is at the disposal of the competitor for advertising. Any advertising shall fit within a rectangle of 4000 cm^2.

3.6 ADVERTISING ON CLOTHING AND PERSONAL EQUIPMENT
In addition to the advertisements carried on the yacht or sailboard, advertisements limited to the organisation(s) advertising on the yacht or sailboard and one or two additional organisations may be displayed on clothing and equipment worn by the crew.

4 Category C

In addition to the advertising permitted by paragraphs 1.8 and 1.9, a yacht competing in a Category C event may display advertising in accordance with special advertising rules. Such rules shall be:

(a) prescribed or approved by the national authority for an event within its jurisdiction;

(b) subject to approval by the IYRU; and

(c) stated in the notice of race and the sailing instructions.

EXPLANATORY SECTION

(Red marginal marks)

Part I – Status of the Rules, Fundamental Rules and Definitions

Fundamental Rules

A   Rendering assistance.
Great importance is attached to racing yachts giving assistance to those in peril. Do not think that somebody else will look after the distressed vessel or person – you must attend the incident unless you are sure your presence is no longer required. See IYRU Case 38.

170

B   Responsibility of a Yacht.
The onus on whether or not a yacht *starts* must rest finally with the yacht and her crew.

C   Fair Sailing.
For an example of this rule applying when *not* racing; a crew might deliberately damage a boat between races during a series. Because you can be disqualified between races it also means you could be disqualified for a whole series. Except for team racing a yacht is not allowed to receive outside help. There was a case where it was suspected that a crew was using a walkie talkie radio with another on shore. If it had been proved, then the yachts would have been disqualified. See also IYRU Case 107.

170

D   Accepting Penalties.
If you are absolutely sure that you have broken a Racing Rule then you should either retire immediately or act under the alternative penalty arrangements if they are in force; but the Racing Rules have no way of stopping a man who has broken the Rules from continuing. In such a case in points racing, you should not interfere with another competitor and force him to get a bad placing when your own placing does not matter. See also Rule 34.

If you really have doubts as to who was right then you should put up your Protest flag. If there was a collision, one or both yachts might have been wrong and it is best to find out so that you will know next time. See also IYRU Cases 2 and 138.

170

Definitions

Definitions – Racing
The rules are in force from the preparatory signal (5-minute gun) until the boat has cleared the finishing line and finishing marks.

Definitions – Starting and Finishing

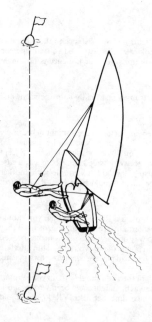

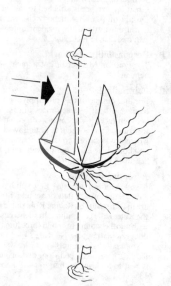

170

This boat has crossed the line to start. See also IYRU Case 34.

Even though the red boat has received her winning gun, she would be disqualified by black because she has not cleared the finishing line.

Definitions – Finishing

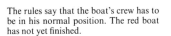

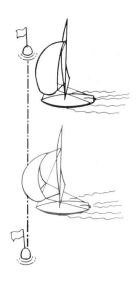

The rules say that the boat's crew has to be in his normal position. The red boat has not yet finished.

Red's spinnaker is not in its normal position and so she has not yet finished. See also page 166 for what happens when a boat touches a finishing mark. A further point to mention is that a race committee is not allowed to override the definition of finishing. See IYRU Case 102.

170

109

Definitions – Luffing and Tacking

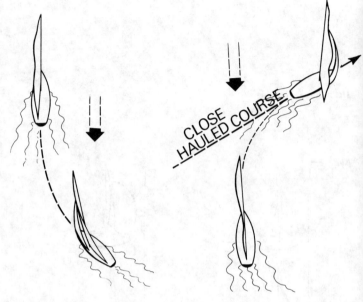

CLOSE HAULED COURSE

170

This yacht is Luffing until she is head to wind. If she continues to turn she is Tacking. See IYRU Case 77.

170

Note that the word 'luff' can also refer to a definite attempt to attack another boat by Luffing. See Rules 38 and 40.

This boat finishes tacking when she reaches a close-hauled course on the new tack, even if the sail is not full because the main-sheet is too loose. Whether the boat has movement through the water or not is irrelevant. See IYRU Case 32.

Definitions – Gybing

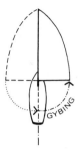

This boat is gybing from the moment when her boom crosses the centreline. The time that the sail is full on the new gybe is when she completes her gybe.

Definitions – Clear Astern, Clear Ahead, Overlap

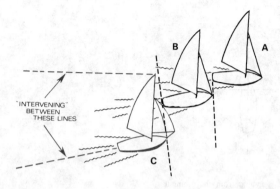

"INTERVENING"
BETWEEN
THESE LINES

182

Watch out because a foresail, a spinnaker or a boomed-out jib could establish an overlap. The so-called 'transom line' is the critical overlap limit, but remember that it passes through the aftermost point of everything.

Yacht B is 'intervening' for the purpose of Rule 38.2(e) (Luffing Rights over two or more yachts), see page 133 and IYRU Case 48.

If yacht B had been overlapping yacht C and yacht A, but on the far side of yacht A, she would not have been an 'intervening' yacht under this definition.

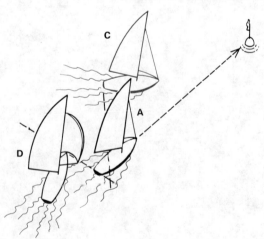

185

Overlap. Yacht A overlaps yacht C. There is no limit to the angle between the courses of yacht A and yacht C, nor their distance apart, for an overlap to be valid, provided that the definition is satisfied. (IYRU Case 21.)

Definitions – Clear Astern, Clear Ahead, Overlap

Clear Astern, Clear Ahead, Overlap. Red has not established an overlap because her spinnaker is not in the normal position.

In this case, the definition says the boats are not overlapped. Rule 36 applies.

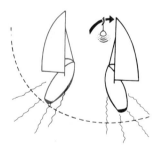

In this case, the boats are overlapped because Rule 42 applies.

Definitions – Windward Yacht, Leeward Yacht

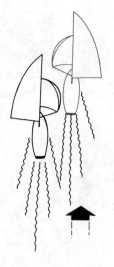

Because these yachts are not on the same tack, neither complies with the definition of windward yacht or leeward yacht.

Here, the definition is not strictly satisfied, but the boat nearer to the wind is the 'windward yacht'.

Definitions – Obstruction

A change of course is only substantial when a boat would lose a substantial amount of ground by altering course. A small fishing buoy, for example, would not cause any obstruction because it would just slide along the side of the boat without stopping it. But a small object such as a post or a buoy and objects such as weed, floating plastic or timber could be an obstruction for the purpose of Rule 38.2(d) (Curtailing a Luff). A racing boat is also an obstruction. See IYRU Cases 91 and 94.

Definitions – Proper Course

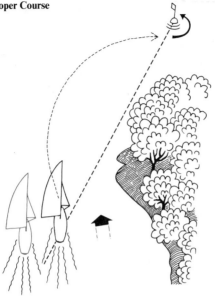

The proper course is not necessarily the shortest course. there can be more than one 'proper course'. The criteria for a proper course is that the yacht should have a valid reason for steering that course and applies it with some con-sistency (IYRU Case 25). The end result has nothing to do with it.

Here, Black can bear away to sail the curved course. See also Rules 38 and 39 and IYRU Cases 62, 97 and 106.

171
171
186

Part II – Organisation and Management

3 – The Sailing Instructions

Many clubs do not take enough trouble over Notices of Race and Sailing Instructions. This often results in confusion, disappointment and bad feeling. It is really very simple for clubs to go through Rules 2 and 3 and make out standard forms which can cover all races.

Rule 3.1 says that the Sailing Instructions shall not alter Rules of Parts I and IV and some other Rules. However, anything else can be changed by them. Committees should be careful not to say too much. See also IYRU Cases 74, 75, 102.

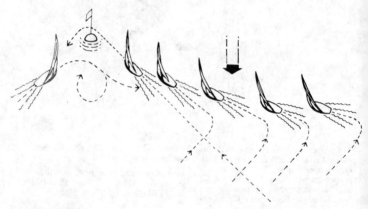

3.2 Contents of the Sailing Instructions.
This drawing illustrates some of the problems for race committees and shows the likely situation when the weather mark is rounded to port.

The disadvantage of port rounding is

that a boat approaching on port tack, even though she may really be leading as Red is here, may not be able to round the mark, and can drop many places. Also, the tendency is to use only the starboard side of the course.

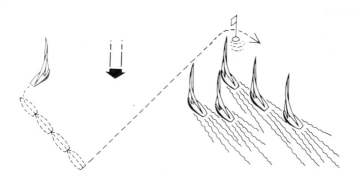

3.2 Contents of the Sailing Instructions.
With starboard rounding, a boat can always get round the mark by standing on

a few lengths, but there are many more protest situations.

3.4 Changes. Unless there is a special procedure laid down in the Sailing Instructions, the Sailing Instructions cannot be varied unless by written amendment.

Oral instructions can easily be wrongly interpreted or even forgotten. See IYRU Case 125.

172

4 – Signals

4.3 In a recall situation, where no gun is fired, there can be no recall. Any visual

signal must be accompanied by a sound signal. (See IYRU Case 134).

172

4.2, 4.4 and **5.1.** Always be prepared so that you can recognise signals, in case the committee stops the race at one of the marks, shortens the course in a special

way, or moves the windward mark as provided for in the programme. See the back cover of this book for quick reference.

4.4 System 2. The White or Yellow, Blue and Red system of starting races, much used in America, is really very simple. It also gives boats one minute extra warn-

ing of the start since each shape is lowered one minute before the next is hoisted.

4.4(d). Signals for Starting a Race. If the race committee realises they have made the preparatory signal either too late or too early, by mistake, they can do one of four things: signal a general recall; postpone the race; or abandon it, and start again; or they can continue with the start.

If they do the latter they must make sure that there is exactly the right time interval between the preparatory signal and the start signal, even if the preparatory was made late or early with reference to the warning signal (ten-minute gun).

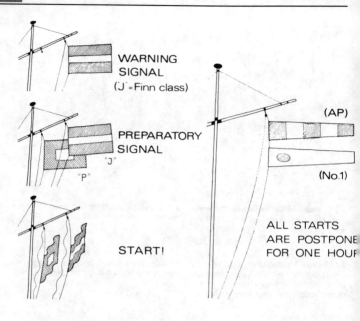

WARNING
SIGNAL
("J"=Finn class)

PREPARATORY
SIGNAL

"J"

"P"

START!

(AP)

(No.1)

ALL STARTS
ARE POSTPONE
FOR ONE HOUR

172

4.5 Visual Starting Signals to Govern.
The timing is made from the flag and not from the gun, bell, whistle or hooter. See the drawing on the left and IYRU Case 70.

172

8 – Recalls
The method of recall to be used must be made clear in the sailing instructions. The onus is on the yacht to see that it not only starts correctly (see also Rule 51.1) but also returns correctly if it is over the line at the starting signal. Unless it prescribes otherwise in the sailing instructions the race committee must make a sound signal for a recall (see IYRU Cases 70 and 134), and support it with a visual signal or a hail.

Part III – General Requirements

19 – Measurement or Rating Certificates

With increasing regularity there are protests concerning these certificates. Owners must satisfy 19.2 in making sure that their yachts comply with the measurement certificates isued to them.

Provided this is satisfied then they cannot be retrospectively invalidated after a race or series is completed. See IYRU Cases 123 and 136.

171

192

22 – Shifting Ballast

Items of the boat's gear shall not be moved about to ballast the boat. Unless in use, gear must remain in its designated place.

Part IV – Right of Way Rules

Section A – Obligations and Penalties

193

This is the most tricky part of the Racing Rules and so we will spend some time in examining cases in detail.

Remember that if you are racing and meet another yacht racing, these Racing Rules apply. It does not matter if the yachts are in different races. If you are not sure that the other yacht is racing then the International Regulations for Preventing Collisions at Sea apply (otherwise known as 'Rule of the Road at Sea'), which all normal shipping has to recognise. These regulations always take precedence if there is doubt.

Take note that the IRPCS should always be enforced in a race between sunset and sunrise.

In order to settle any damage claims the result of a yacht racing protest is normally binding on two yachts racing. If one or both yachts are not racing then liability depends on the 'Rule of the Road at Sea'.

Appendix 9 summarises the important and salient points of the IRPCS to assist competitors with this knowledge of the regulations. See also IYRU Case 137.

173

31 – Rule Infringement

Before you go afloat you should study the Sailing Instructions very carefully (see Rule 3) because you can be disqualified if you fail to keep any of the special rules for a particular race. For example, you may be required to carry some special flag in your rigging, or you may be required to wear lifejackets, or there may be some special starting instructions such as the one-minute rule, or you may have to carry extra buoyancy.

173

32 – Serious Damage

32.1 Avoiding Collisions. If the right-of-way yacht tries to avoid a collision and fails, and this collision results in 'serious damage', then she is in the clear.

But the problem is to decide what is 'serious damage'. There is not much that cannot be patched up quickly on a dinghy and it is the duty of the yacht in the wrong to make amends as soon as possible, but keelboats can do more damage to each other. On international race courses, the result of the race is much more important than the equip-ment. The collision only gives a more accurate indication of a protest situation.

IYRU Case 36 gives as a criteria for 'serious damage' that consideration must be given to the extent and the cost of repair relative to the size and value of the yacht; whether it was feasible or prudent for her to continue to race; and whether the damage markedly affected her speed and materially prejudiced her finishing position. (See also IYRU Cases 51 and 53).

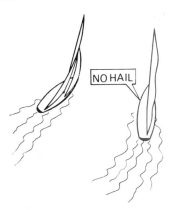

NO HAIL

32.2 Hailing. No hail from Red tacking on to starboard may cause her to be disqualified for an unforeseen alteration of course.

33 – Contact between Yachts Racing

If the contact is minor and unavoidable no action by either yacht is necessary, but beware – there are several interpretations of 'minor and unavoidable'. Should a third yacht make a protest under Rule 33.2 about the incident then it will be the job of the Protest Committee to decide. Further to this, a yacht which wishes to protect herself may make a protest under 33. If the Protest Committee decide at the hearing that contact was indeed minor and unavoidable then the protest may be withdrawn under Rule 68.9.

IYRU Case 141 gives an interpretation of 'minor and unavoidable'. The circumstances are usually associated with little or no wind, with concentrations of yachts with no steerage way. Where yachts have steerage way contact is usually considered avoidable. Minor contact implies no damage. The test of avoidability should not be applied at the instant before contact. Events leading up to the incident should be taken into consideration. It is a difficult interpretation to make and is often disputed; when two yachts contact and agree it is minor and unavoidable a third yacht looking on may not.

174

Section B – Principal Right of Way Rules and their Limitations.

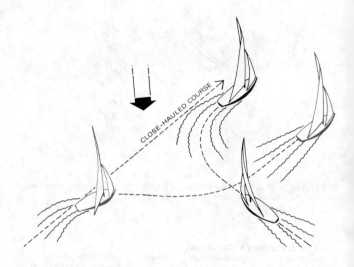

175
176
177

174

35 – Limitations on Altering Course

Apart from the references mentioned below, IYRU Cases 36, 51, 86 and 115 are relevant.

■ **35 and 41.** Red has borne away to pass under Black's stern and Black decides to tack to cover. In order to avoid infringing Rules 35 or 41, Black must not tack until she is past the Red yacht's course. There may be some doubt as to the actual direction of the course, and in this case the onus will be on Black to show that Red did not have to alter course further because of Black while Black's tack was in progress. See also IYRU Cases 23 and 52.

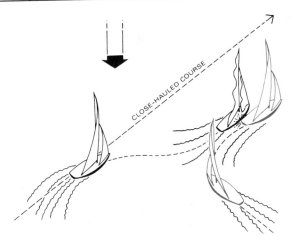

CLOSE-HAULED COURSE

■ **35** and **41.** Here Black bore away to pass under Red's stern. When Red saw this she tacked. There was a collision and Red was wrong under Rule 41 (Tacking yacht keeps clear).

Rule 35 ceased to apply when Red passed head to wind and thus stopped being the right-of-way boat.

Red became right-of-way yacht again when she completed her tack, but in such a case Black would not have to *begin* to take avoiding action until Red's tack was completed. See also IYRU Cases 10 and 23.

174

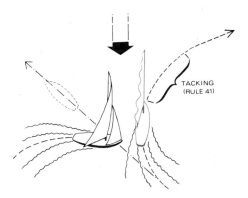

TACKING
(RULE 41)

■ **35** and **41.** If the Red yacht luffs head to wind she can be disqualified under Rule 35 because Black had already altered course to avoid Red.

If she goes further and tacks, she can be disqualified under both Rules 35 and 41, depending on where the incident actually occurred. See also IYRU Cases 10, 23 and 53.

174
182

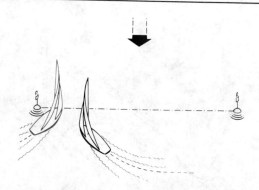

■ **35.** The Red yacht, on port tack, has to remember that starboard tack yachts like Black have the right to luff on to a proper course to start after the starting gun. Note that there is no proper course before the starting signal.

The timing of the signal and the yacht's start can be quite far apart. Before the start, luffs (under Rule 40) have to be slow. But Black's luff here can be fast because the yachts are on opposite tacks.

If this situation had occurred after Black had started it would be the same as if the marks were not there. Black could not luff to prevent Red keeping clear.

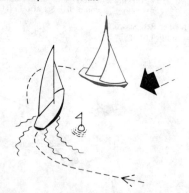

35. Red takes the mark rather wide and tacks. Black rounds tighter and can touch Red. Red is wrong under Rule 36 (Port and Starboard Rule).

If the buoy has not been there, Black would be wrong under Rule 35 for obstructing Red who would otherwise have been able to keep clear. However, the final clause to Rule 35 (when rounding a mark) makes an exception in this case.

■ **35.** If a right of way yacht alters course in such a way that the disadvantaged yacht in spite of prompt avoiding action still cannot keep clear by her own efforts then the right of way yacht infringes Rule 35. See IYRU Case 129.

36 – Opposite Tacks – Basic Rule – Port and Starboard

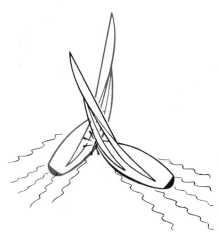

Port and Starboard incidents without contact are very common. There is no requirement in the Rules for the onus to be on the port tack yacht to prove he was clear of the starboard tack yacht, but conversely there is nothing in the Rules to suggest that the starboard tack yacht should hit the port tack yacht. See IYRU Case 113.

IYRU Cases 6, 35, 36, 37, 45, 51, 52, 68, 93, 112 and 113 contain further interpretations of this rule.

177
174
175
176
177
180
184
188

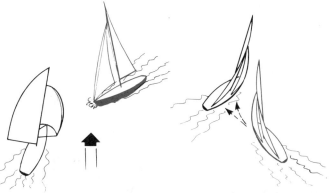

■ **36.** Black has the wind coming from the starboard side and Red the wind from the port side. Thus Red should give way to Black.

35 and **36.** Red must not luff to try to hit Black, who would otherwise have been able to keep clear. This case comes under Rule 35. See also IYRU Cases 36 and 52.

174
175

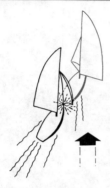 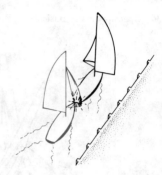

183
186

■ **36.** Even though Black is overtaking Red, the definition of 'clear astern' is not valid because they are on opposite tacks and so Rule 36 applies. Red must give way because Black is sailing on starboard tack.

■ **36** and **42.2.** Here they are subject to Rule 42 and Red must keep clear even if Black gybes because she is within two of her overall lengths of an obstruction. See also Rule 37.2 and IYRU Cases 5 and 68.

37 – Same Tack – Basic Rules

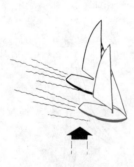 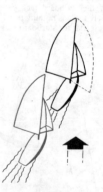

171
176
178
179
180
182
188

37.1 When Overlapped. Red is windward boat and therefore has to keep clear of Black.

Further examples are covered in IYRU Cases 3, 25, 48, 50, 54 and 68.

37.2. When not Overlapped. Red must keep clear and must not sail into Black's stern if they are on the same tack. See also IYRU Case 86.

37.3. Transitional. Before the start the Red yacht comes from astern with better speed. Red obtained the overlap too close to Black, who was not given enough room by Red to luff clear. Black is right under Rule 37.3. See also IYRU Cases 114 and 116.

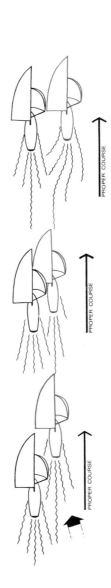

180

37.3. Transitional. In this special case Red has overtaken Black but has given too little room for Black to be able to luff and keep clear, because Black's stern will swing to port as she luffs. See also IYRU Cases 11 and 46.

178

37.1 and **37.3. When Overlapped and ▶ Transitional.** The Black yacht is overtaking. From the moment that Black gains an overlap the Red yacht becomes the 'windward yacht'. She must then start to luff far enough so that Black does not touch her boom, but she need not luff any further because Black must not luff above her proper course. See IYRU Cases 11, 27, 46 and 106.

171
178

38 – Same Tack – Luffing after Clearing the Starting Line

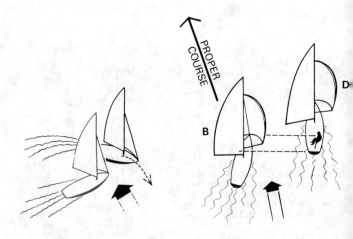

38.1. Luffing rights. Red is overtaking. Black has the right to luff because she was ahead and is now to leeward, and is still ahead of Red's 'mast abeam' position.

IYRU Cases 3, 4, 48, 58, and 62 are relevant.

38.1. Luffing rights. B is overtaking D but on a course which is slightly higher than the proper course. We cannot talk about luffing here, but nevertheless D's helmsman should call 'Mast abeam!', and thus B is obliged to turn back on to the proper course and may not luff again as long as this overlap exists. See also IYRU Case 24 and Rule 40 for this situation before starting.

**178
179
180
181
182
183
186**

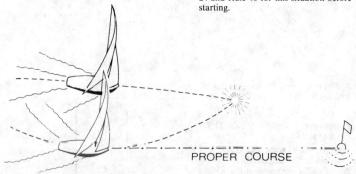

PROPER COURSE

171

38.2(a). Proper Course Limitations. Red establishes her overlap by diving through the Black yacht's lee but must not luff above her proper course whilst the overlap lasts. If there is a dispute about what

is the proper course then the Black yacht must keep clear. See also IYRU Cases 25 and 106, and also our interpretation of Proper Course.

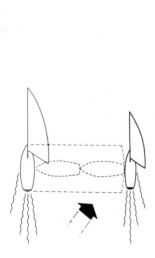

38.2(b). Overlap Limitations. The measurement of the two yachts' length distance is taken from hull to hull as shown, but this maximum limit only applies to Rule 38 (Luffing).

Rule 39 (Bearing away) has a three length limit.

38.2(b). Overlap Limitations. Black's overlap starts from the moment when she completes her tack. Here the black yacht overlaps the Red.

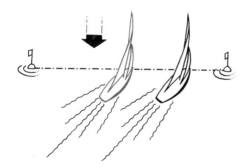

38.2(b). Overlap Limitations. At the start the overlap begins at the time when the leading boat actually crosses the starting line.

38.2(b). Overlap Limitations. Black is overtaking Red and as soon as her mast goes forward of Red's helmsman, she may gybe and then gains luffing rights. If Black was overtaking on the same gybe as Red, then she could gain her luffing rights by doing two quick gybes. But see IYRU Case 35.

38.2(b). Overlap Limitations. The overlap starts from the moment the yachts have completed their gybes and therefore there can be no question of luffing rights until this moment. See IYRU Case 62.

PROPER
COURSE

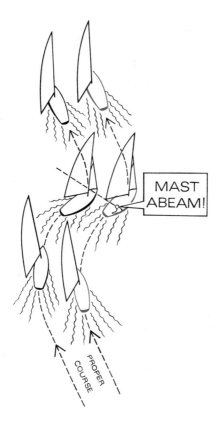

MAST ABEAM!

PROPER COURSE

38.2(c). Hailing to Stop or Prevent a Luff.
Remember to call 'Mast abeam!' or something similar, because this is the only way you can take away the luffing rights of the leeward yacht. After this the leeward yacht must bear away on to her proper course. She can only regain luffing rights if she breaks the overlap by drawing clear ahead or more than two lengths abeam, and then re-establishes it again with her mast forward of the windward boat's helmsman. See also Rule 40 and IYRU Cases 3, 4 and 101.

178
181

131

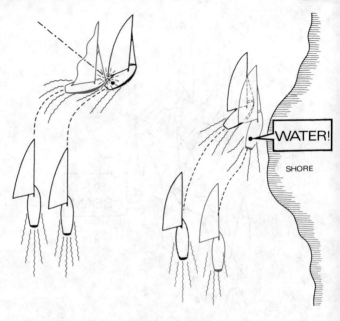

WATER!

SHORE

171

38.2(c). Hailing to Stop or Prevent a Luff. Red starts to luff correctly but hits Black when she is obviously behind the mast abeam position. Red is wrong. There is no doubt because the position of the collision proves it.

181
182

However, let us take a slightly different situation where Red has a greater overlap on Black when she starts luffing. Rule 38.2(d) says clearly that when there is doubt then Black (windward yacht) must hail because the helmsman of Black is in the best position to see. Once Black has hailed 'Mast abeam' Red luffs at her risk, or disputes the call by Protesting. There is a big difference between continuing the luff and actual contact. See IYRU Cases 48 and 99.

38.2(d). Curtailing a Luff. Black is entitled to luff and does so in this case. Red can now stop the luff by calling 'Water'. Black does not have to return to her proper course but need only just give enough room, because Red has not reached 'Mast abeam!' position. See IYRU Case 106.

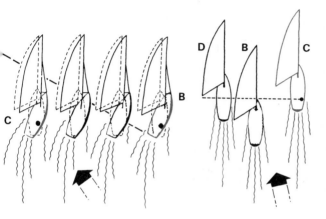

38.2(e). Luffing Rights over Two or More Yachts. In this instance C has luffed the others, but because of her turn, loses luffing rights over B. B can call 'Mast Abeam!' and force C to go back on her proper course. See also IYRU Case 4.

38.2(e). Luffing Rights over Two or More Yachts. Yacht B is 'intervening'. C must respond to a luff from D, who has rights over B and C. C must also allow room for B even though B may have no luffing rights of her own over C.

181

39 – Same Tack – Sailing Below a Proper Course After Starting

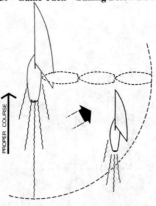

■ **39.** Black is inside a distance of three yachts' lengths from Red. Red must not bear away from her proper course to interfere with Black if it is a free leg of the course.

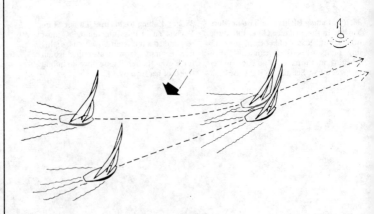

■ **39** and **37.1.** If the leg is to windward, Red may bear away towards Black's course, but if she touches she will be disqualified under Rule 37.1. If a tack will have to be made to reach the next mark this is evidence that the leg is to 'windward'. See IYRU Case 106.

171

40 – Same Tack – Luffing before Clearing the Starting Line

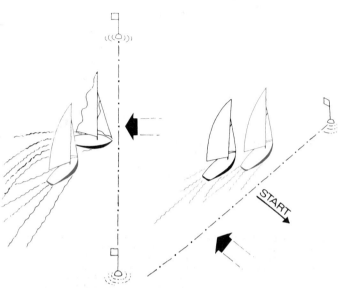

■ **40.** Provided Black is ahead of 'Mast abeam!' position she can luff slowly head to wind. She cannot be forced to bear away at any time before or after the starting signal. See also page 124 top drawing. IYRU Case 115 is relevant in a match racing situation.

■ **40.** As long as Black is not ahead of the mast abeam position he may only luff slowly to a close hauled course. She must give Red enough time and room to keep clear. See IYRU Case 24.

178
175

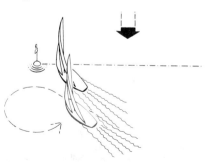

■ **40.** Red must not luff above close-hauled to squeeze round the mark, when she is aft of 'Mast abeam!'. See also Rule 43.3.

41 – Changing Tack – Tacking and Gybing

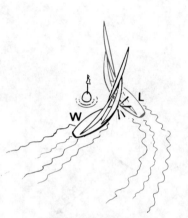

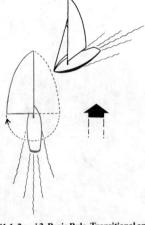

180
182

41.1, 2 and **3. Basic Rule, Transitional and Onus.** Red tacks on to starboard and must have completed her tack before she can claim right-of-way over Black. Black does not have to begin to give way until Red's tack is complete. See also the example on page 145 (top left) and IYRU Cases 32, 53 and 58.

41.1, 2 and **3. Basic Rule, Transitional and Onus.** Red must complete her gybe before she can force Black to alter course. Here Red has gybed too late to gain right-of-way over Black, because Black has no possibility of being able to keep clear. In case of doubt the onus of proof is on Red. In practice this means that Red must have a witness from a third yacht.

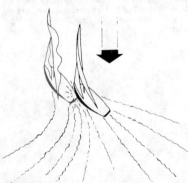

170

41.2. Transitional. Red is coming on port tack and is tacking on to starboard tack. Red has only just completed her tack. Black does not have to start to luff until after this moment and is therefore right. See Definition and IYRU Case 32.

Note: 41.3. Onus. It is clearly stated in this Rule, and applies also to other Rules, that you have to 'satisfy the race committee' that your manoeuvre was correct. Unless you can succeed in this your whole case will fail.

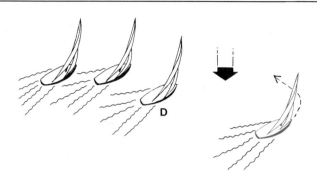

41.2. Transitional. In this situation the Red yacht tacks but there is no possibility of D being able to clear Red after Red has completed her tack because of the proximity of the other yachts. Red has not satisfied Rule 41.2. If the Red yacht was to tack on to starboard she would have to bear away astern of D.

41.2, Transitional and **42.** In this situation if the Black yacht (on the right) tacks, the Red yacht can only bear away (and give room to B and A under Rule 42 if they have an overlap). This is because there is no time for the Red yacht to hail B and A for room to tack themselves before a collision would occur with Black.

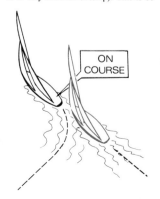

ON COURSE

41.2. Transitional. This situation is covered by Rule 41.2. A hail from Black when she has completed her tack will clarify the moment when she gains the right to force Red to start avoiding a collision. Red does not have to start any avoiding action until Black has completed her tack.

137

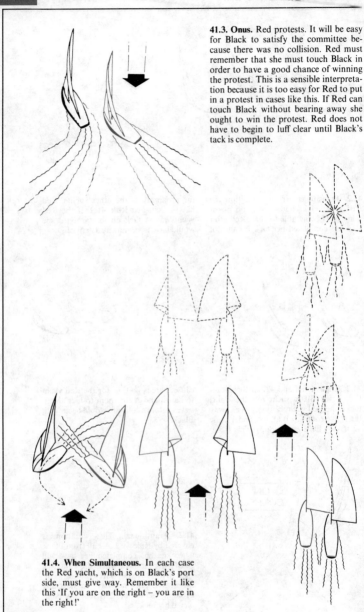

41.3. Onus. Red protests. It will be easy for Black to satisfy the committee because there was no collision. Red must remember that she must touch Black in order to have a good chance of winning the protest. This is a sensible interpretation because it is too easy for Red to put in a protest in cases like this. If Red can touch Black without bearing away she ought to win the protest. Red does not have to begin to luff clear until Black's tack is complete.

41.4. When Simultaneous. In each case the Red yacht, which is on Black's port side, must give way. Remember it like this 'If you are on the right – you are in the right!'

Section C – Marks and Obstructions and Exceptions to Section B

All Rules in this section cover special cases. When these cases apply they override all the basic rules which precede them in Section B of Part IV, with the exception of Rule 35 which has its own limitations.

Section A (31–34) rules always apply and do not describe the sort of yacht-to-yacht situations covered in Section B (35–41) and Section C (42–46).

42 – Rounding or Passing Marks and Obstructions
This is one of the most important rules as it is the one that is involved most frequently. It is set out in four parts.

■ **42.1.** Instructions for rounding and passing marks and obstructions when *overlapped* either as an inside or an outside yacht.

■ **42.2.** Instructions for rounding and passing marks and obstruction when yachts are *not overlapped* either when clear ahead or clear astern.

■ **42.3.** Limitations on establishing an overlap and Limitations when the obstruction is a continuing one.

■ **42.4.** The special case of room at a starting mark.

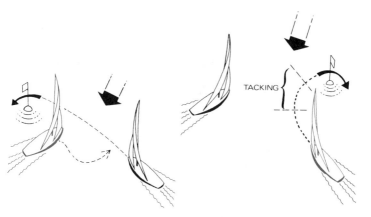

TACKING

■ **42(a).** This clause says that Rule 42.1(a) does not apply in this situation because the two boats are sailing to windward on opposite tacks. Rule 36 applies, and so Black does not have to give room to Red to round a mark inside her.

■ **42(a).** Red cannot claim room during her tacking manoeuvre though she may have rights both before and after it.

It is exactly the same as if they were on the open sea with no mark anywhere near. If Red were to tack then Rule 41 would apply.

42 – Rounding or Passing Marks and Obstructions

42.1 – When overlapped

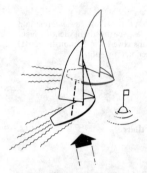

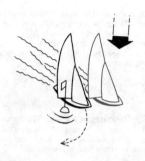

180
183

42.1(a). An Outside Yacht. Red shall give room to Black, assuming Black made her overlap in time. See also Rule 42.3 for the limits to claiming overlaps, and IYRU Case 50.

42.1(a). An Outside Yacht. Black must have enough room to be able to gybe without being obstructed by Red. Red must still keep clear even if Black's gybe breaks the overlap. See also IYRU Case 5.

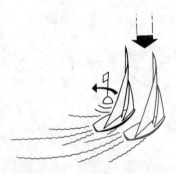

186

42.1(a). An Outside Yacht. Black, the inside overlapping yacht, must have room to be able to tack. If Black's genoa touched Red when it was freed off for the tacking, for example, Red would not have given her enough room. See also IYRU Case 40 for an interpretation of the word 'room'.

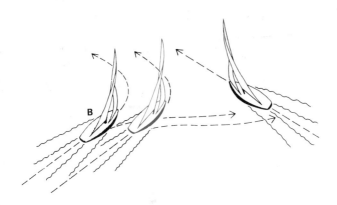

42.1(a). An Outside Yacht, and **43.** The starboard tack yacht is an obstruction. Red can elect to tack or to bear away. If the latter, she has to give room to yacht B who is overlapping 'inside'. IYRU Cases 6 and 20.

184
188

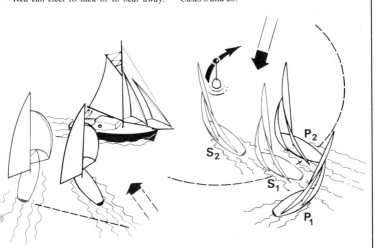

42.1(a). An Outside Yacht. The yacht not racing is crossing the course and Red must give Black room to pass on the same side as herself.

Also when approaching a mark Red must give Black room even though both yachts are on widely differing courses. See also IYRU Case 21.

Rule 42.1(a). Approaching a starboard hand windward mark, P passed close astern of S and tacked on to starboard completing it within two lengths of the mark. The two lengths determinative of Rule 42.3(a)(ii) does not therefore apply. P can claim room to round inside S provided she gains an overlap before the start of S's rounding manoeuvre.

185

page

183
184

Rule 42

*For official rules text
see BLACK section*

42.1(a). An Outside Yacht. When a yacht comes abreast of a mark but is more than two lengths from it, and when her alteration of course towards the mark results in a yacht previously clear astern becoming overlapped inside her, Rule 42.1(a) requires her to give room to that yacht. See IYRU Cases 5 and 127.

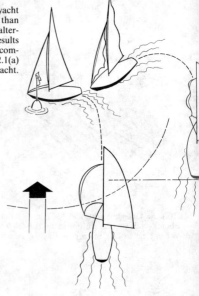

42.1(b). An Outside Yacht. It may sometimes happen that, when sailing in strong currents, one or both yachts may drift outside the two-length zone before rounding. If only the inside yacht drifts outside the circle then the overlap still technically exists. If the outside yacht drifts outside then the overlap has to be re-established.

CURRENT

42.1(b). An Outside Yacht. Black has an overlap in time. The gybe breaks the overlap but this rule says that in this situation Black can still claim room to round inside.

42.1(b). Taking an Inside Yacht the Wrong Side of a Mark. If you wish to take a windward yacht to the wrong side you may do it, but you must (i) have luffing rights and (ii) be outside the two yacht-length circle. As soon as you reach this point, and the weather yacht still has an overlap, Rule 42.1(b) applies and you must give him room.

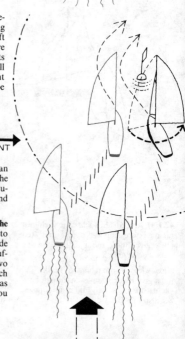

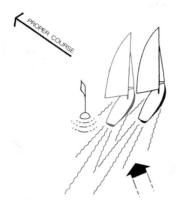

42.1(e). An Inside Yacht. Red, unless she has luffing rights, must gybe on to her proper course. Black can choose what she does. This rule overrides Rule 37. See also IYRU Case 62.

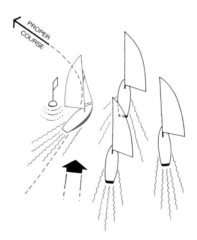

42.1(e). An Inside Yacht. Red must gybe on to the new proper course at the earliest opportunity. She is not allowed to continue and force the others to keep clear. This Rule overrides Rule 36.

42.2 – When not Overlapped

42.2(a). A Yacht Clear Astern. Red must keep clear even though she now has an overlap because this was not made in time (see Rule 42.3(a)). Neither can Red claim her starboard tack rights.

42.2(a). A Yacht Clear Astern. Black, who is clear ahead, has the right to gybe. This is part of the rounding manoeuvre and so Red must stay clear until Black has gybed and cleared the mark.

See also the top, right drawing page 126 and IYRU Case 68.

This clause covers the case of a gybe. A tack is covered in paragraph (c).

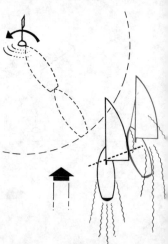

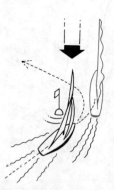

42.2(c). A Yacht Clear Ahead, and **41.** Red is clear ahead but cannot claim room to tack because 42.2(c) says that in this case Rule 41 is the correct rule. See IYRU Case 26.

42.2(a). A Yacht Clear Astern. Black is allowed to make a normal smooth rounding. She is within a radius of two yacht lengths of the mark and is also clear ahead of Red, and so she does not have to give room when she is altering course to round the mark.

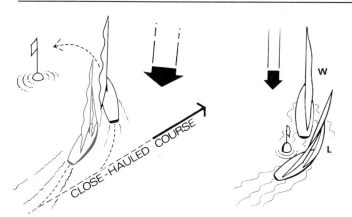

42.2(b) and (c). A Yacht Clear Astern. If Black thinks she is far enough ahead to be able to tack and clear Red without causing her to alter course, she can do so. Red must not then luff above a close-hauled course to prevent Black from clearing her.

This is really a small extension of Rule 35. It means that the mark should be ignored.

42.2(c). A Yacht Clear Ahead. The course is from a reach to a reach. W luffs nearly head to wind. L cannot get between W and the mark because of Rule 42.2(a). After L has steered to pass under W's stern then W can tack and continue.

42.3. Limitations

42.3(a). Limitation on Establishing an Overlap. We all know how yachts surge back and forth relative to each other on waves. This can be quite dangerous when claiming room at a mark and so you have to claim your overlap before the leading yacht is within two lengths of the mark. This gives her a fair chance of giving room.

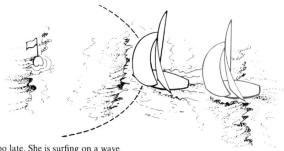

Red is too late. She is surfing on a wave at twice the speed of Black who has no chance of giving room.

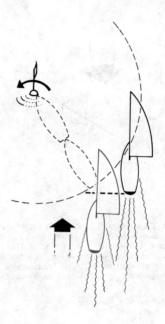

42.3(a). Limitation on Establishing an Overlap. Red is not within the limit distance of two yacht lengths of the mark when she alters course, so she cannot refuse to give Black room.

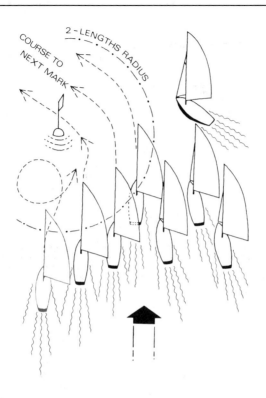

42.3(a)(i). Limitation on Establishing an Overlap. Even though Red has established an overlap in proper time on the next yacht, the latter may not be able to give room because of the delay in response from the outside yachts. If she has been given too little room, Red ought not to risk making a Protest under Rule 42.1(a). See also IYRU Case 27.

178

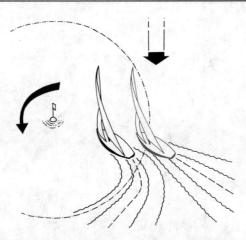

NOT 42.3(a)(ii). Limitation on Establishing an Overlap. In this case 42.1(a) applies since there is no question of obtaining an overlap from **clear astern**.

Black's tack has been completed within the circle. The circle can therefore be forgotten and Black can try to obtain room under 42.1(a) or 37.1.

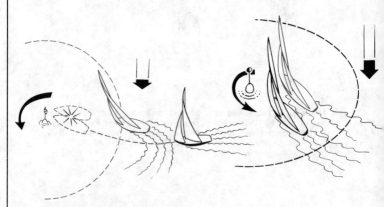

42.3(a)(ii). Limitation on Establishing an Overlap. If Red completes her tack within the two length circle Black would have right of way before the tack (Rule 36), during the tack (Rule 41) and after the tack (Rule 37). And as she establishes her overlap whilst Red is completing her tack she obtains room at the mark under Rule 42.1(a).

But if Red had completed her tack outside the two length circle then as long as she satisfied her requirements under Rule 41 Black would not have room at the mark.

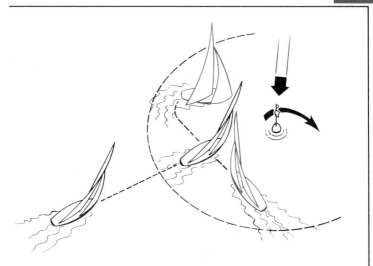

42.3(a)(ii). Limitation on Establishing an Overlap. Red completes her tack within two lengths of the mark. Therefore Black can ask for room between Red and the mark.

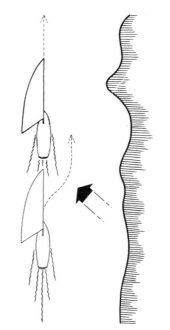

42.3(b). Limitation when an Obstruction is a Continuing One. This is an awkward Rule to interpret. Presumably the leading yacht is already as close to the obstruction as she thinks she can go with safety. Therefore it is difficult for the overtaking yacht to show that she can go safely closer. See IYRU Case 69.

The two-lengths limit does not apply so it is dangerous to try for an overlap under this rule. If an overlap is established correctly, Black cannot luff Red ashore.

188

149

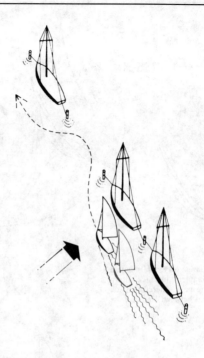

42.3(b). Limitation when an Obstruction is a Continuing One. Black must be careful when arriving at a break in the obstruction. This is Red's chance to establish an overlap.

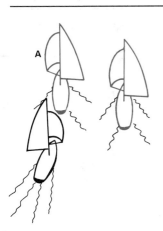

NOT 42.3(a). Limitation on Establishing an Overlap. This case was the subject of IYRU Case 45. Black, on starboard tack, has right-of-way over the other two under Rule 36. The port tack yacht A is not a 'continuing obstruction' with respect to the other.

See also IYRU Case 67 for another situation where 42.3(b) does apply, and also IYRU Case 35.

177

187
176

42.4 – At a Starting Mark Surrounded by Navigable Water

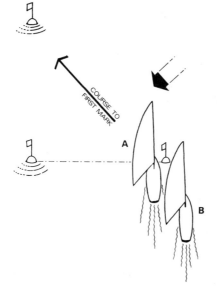

■ **42.4.** As soon as the starting gun has fired, A must bear away onto the course for the first mark and must not squeeze B out by sailing higher than this.

If there is still not enough room for B then A is not obliged to sail lower than the course to the first mark. 42.1 does not apply but 37.1 does. See IYRU Case 54.

178

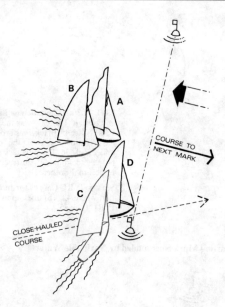

COURSE TO NEXT MARK

CLOSE-HAULED COURSE

178

■ **42.4.** Yacht C can neither claim room between yacht D and the mark before the starting gun nor afterwards. Rule 37.1 also applies.

Yacht A, which is ahead of 'Mast Abeam', is head to wind and has the right

to do this also after the starting gun has fired because yacht B has plenty of room between her and the mark. See IYRU Case 54.

This rule is often called the 'anti-barging rule'.

43 – Close-hauled, Hailing for Room to Tack at Obstructions

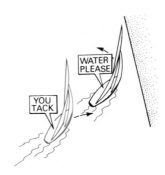

43.1 and .2. Hailing and Responding.
Black can no longer continue in safety.
Red must start to tack immediately she
hears Black's hail. Black must start to
tack before Red has completed her tack.

43.1 and .2(b). Hailing and Responding.
Black has the right to call for water, but
Red can reply 'You tack!', and then she
is obliged to keep clear of Black. Black
must start to tack immediately after
Red's reply hail.

Red must remember that in the case of
a protest she will have to prove that she
has kept clear of Black during this
manoeuvre.

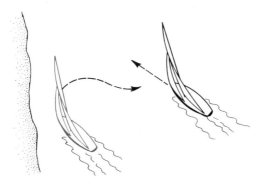

43.1. Hailing. In this case Red is easily
able to tack and keep clear of Black. She
has no right to call for water. She only
has the right to call for water when she
is certain that she cannot clear Black
either by passing ahead, or by bearing
away under her stern. See IYRU Cases
80 and 117.

188

153

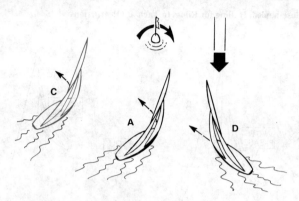

43.1. Hailing. Yacht A shall hail for room
to tack and yacht C must keep clear.

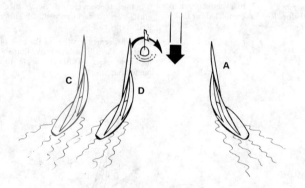

43.1. Hailing. Here yacht D shall hail and
yacht C must tack, not because she can-

not lay the mark (43.3), but because
yacht A is coming in on starboard tack.

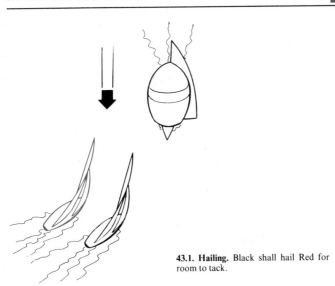

43.1. Hailing. Black shall hail Red for room to tack.

43.3 – When the Obstruction is Also a Mark

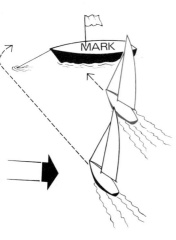

43.3(a). If Black can fetch the mark she need not give Red room to tack unless Red cannot avoid a collision either with the mark or with Black. Then Red should hail a second time and immediately she is clear she must retire.

If Red had been slightly more to windward she would have been able to hail for water because of the mooring rope which is not part of the mark (see definitions).

155

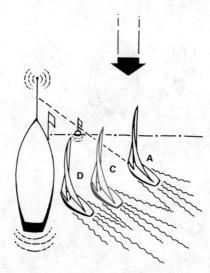

43.3(b).
Case 1. The line is between two buoys. The starting yacht is not a starting mark.

In this situation yacht D can hail yacht C for room to tack at any time. Yacht C can only hail yacht A for room to tack because of the starting yacht and not to pass the right side of the starting mark. If yacht D were not there yacht C might have been forced to sail over the line between the mark and the starting yacht before she could claim room.

43.3(a)
Case 2. The starting yacht is a starting mark, as is the inner limit mark, which has a 'required side' only after a yacht starts (i.e. first cuts the line after the gun).

Neither yacht D nor yacht C can claim room to tack from yacht A when the obstruction is a starting mark and that includes the ground tackle.

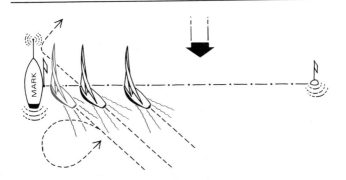

43.3(a). The starting yacht forms one end of the line and is therefore a mark of the course and has a required side as soon as a yacht starts. Red must foresee this situation and pull out of the line in time.

The middle yacht may not be able to claim room for the ground tackle which is also an obstruction.

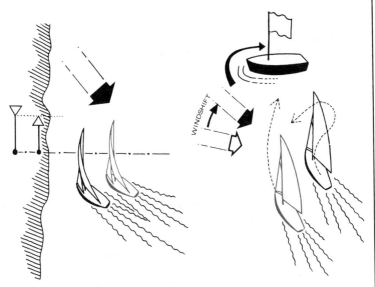

43.3(b). In the case of a starting line transit which is completely on the shore, both before and after the start Black can hail Red for water to tack because the shore is an obstruction.

43.3(c). After Red has declined Black's call to tack, the latter bears away in order to tack and pass under Red's stern. Now the wind shifts and Red cannot any longer lay the mark. Because of her refusal Red must immediately retire.

157

44 – Returning to Start

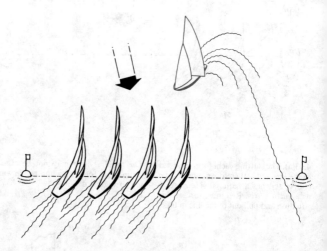

■ **44.1.** Even though a yacht which has started too early is on starboard tack, she has to keep clear of all others – even port tack yachts.

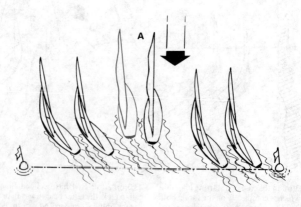

■ **44.1** Red has started too early and luffs into the wind in order to slow down so that she can drop back and start again.

But if she affects yacht A, then yacht A will have to respond and Red will be disqualified.

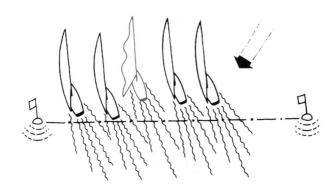

■ **44.1.** The Red yacht has started too early but the only thing she can do is let go the jib and the mainsail. She can slow down by backing the sails if she can do it without affecting the other yachts. As soon as she lets the sheets go, to slow down, she has begun her manoeuvre to return to the line, and she must keep clear of other yachts.

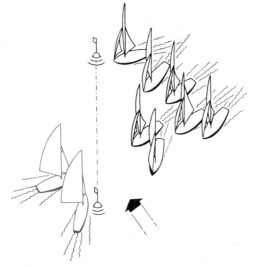

■ **44.1.** As soon as the starting signal is made, the Red yachts, who are on the wrong side of the line, must keep clear. Before the starting signal has fired they have right-of-way because they are on starboard tack, but as they have to gybe or tack before they can start, and while making this manoeuvre keep clear, it can be dangerous to start in this way.

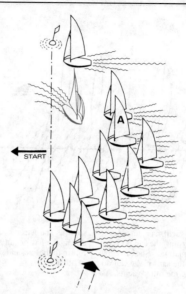

■ **44.1(b).** Even though she has regained her starboard tack rights, the Red yacht must tack or bear away because the rule says that she has to give yacht A, for example, ample room and opportunity to keep clear. It will be impossible for yacht A to comply in this situation.

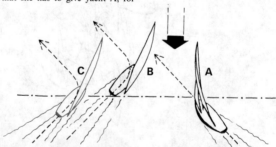

189

■ **44.2.** Yacht B has started too early and, because of the starboard tack yacht, she has to call upon yacht C for room to tack. Yacht B has the right to do this because she is not yet returning to make her restart. After tacking she can then begin to slow down as long as this does not affect yacht A or yacht C. See IYRU Case 81.

189

45.1. Keeping Clear after Touching a Mark. If you are exonerating yourself after touching a mark, you must stay well clear of non-penalised yachts until you are on a proper course to the next mark. Rule 42.1(a) is not applied.

But yachts making a normal rounding may not take advantage of the offending yachts; they must round in the normal way and assume their proper course. Rule 35 applies. See IYRU Case 81.

46 – Person Overboard; Yacht Anchored, Aground or Capsized

■ **46.1.** You have to keep clear of a capsized dinghy. Under the Rules it is the same as if it was an obstruction.

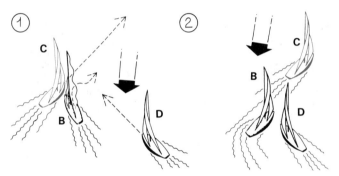

■ **46.** Yacht B on starboard was hit by yacht C on port, and knocked on to the other tack. Yacht B is now nearly stopped on port tack and is hit by yacht D who is on starboard. Yachts 'out of control' are not covered by this Rule. Yacht B is not wrong and should Protest against yacht C.

Hailing situations summarized

1. Obligatory hailing situations
   (a) Hail for room to tack at an obstruction (43.1).
   (b) Hailing to Stop or Prevent a Luff (38.2(c)) (i) Mast abeam or (ii) Obstruction.
   (c) A yacht anchored or aground shall indicate the fact to a yacht in danger of fouling her. A hail would be the usual method (46.4).
   (d) When Alternative Penalties can be taken, an immediate hail by the protesting yacht gives the protested yacht a chance to exonerate herself (Appendix 3 (1.3) (68.2).
   (e) A right-of-way yacht must hail if she makes an alteration of course that may not be foreseen by another yacht (32.2).
   (f) A Protesting yacht shall try to inform another yacht that she intends to Protest. Hailing would be the preferred method (68.2).
2. Recommended hailing situations
   (a) Any situation or manoeuvre where a hail would clarify or support one's case e.g. in the establishment or termination of an overlap at a mark or obstruction (42.1(f)).
   (b) Loss of crew overboard (46.1(a)).

Part V – Other Sailing Rules

50 – Ranking as a Starter

Sailing about in the vicinity of the starting line does not mean that you have to be on the pre-start side of the starting line

to rank as a starter. See IYRU Cases 34 and 111.

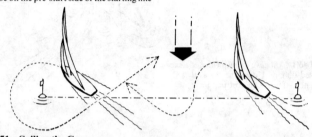

51 – Sailing the Course

51. Sailing the Course. During a normal start a yacht which is over the line early can restart like yacht D. However, if the 'round-the-ends' Rule 51.1(c) is invoked and Code flag 'I' was flown, as frequently happens after a general recall, then a yacht which is over the line will have to return like yacht A.

51.1(a). Sailing the Course. Inner and Outer limit marks described in the Sailing Instructions as being part of the Finishing line must be either on the line or on the course side of the line. If a limit mark is laid or drifts to the post-course side of the Finishing line, it should be disregarded. See IYRU Case 124.

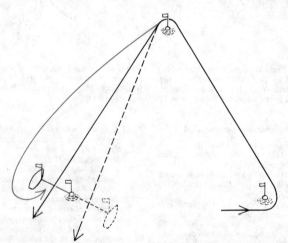

51.1(a). Sailing the Course. If the sailing instructions say that you should finish by leaving the committee boat to port and, for example, if they put the committee

yacht on the wrong side of the mark, you should follow the finishing definition exactly. See IYRU Case 102.

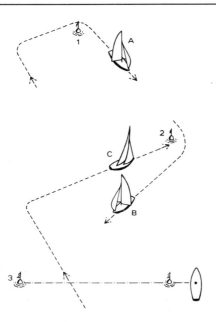

51.3. Sailing the Course. Both marks 1 and 2 are marks of the course for yacht A.

B has just rounded mark 2 and therefore mark 1 is no longer considered as a mark for her.

C has not yet rounded mark 1 and therefore she can please herself which side of mark 2 she goes. She can touch it without infringing these rules (see Rule 52).

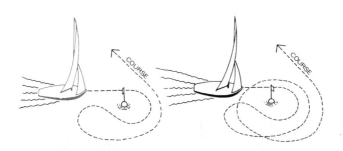

51.2 and **4. Sailing the Course.** Red has rounded incorrectly. Black is right. You have to unwind yourself before rounding properly.

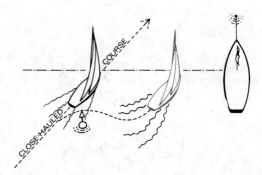

51.3. Sailing the Course. A starting mark first has a 'required side' when a yacht starts (i.e. first cuts the line), but it must not be touched even before the start.

A starting limit mark first has a 'required side' when a yacht is approaching the line to start.

This definition is not clear unless it means 'after the starting signal' because a yacht does not 'approach the line to start' until then.

51.3. Sailing the Course. Black must be correct because she has passed the limit mark on the required side when approaching the line to start.

Red is wrong because the mark had already been passed before her 'approach to the line to start'.

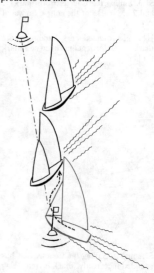

51.5. Sailing the Course. Red, who has crossed the finishing line, still has to keep clear of the starboard tack boats. She can go under their sterns and still maintains her finishing position because she has already finished. She may clear the line in any direction.

52 – Touching a Mark

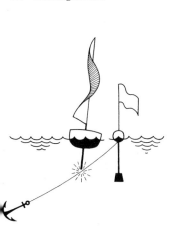

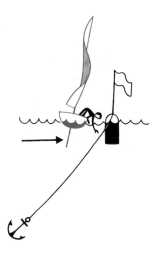

52 and **definition – mark.** You can touch the buoy rope with the keel without infringing Rule 52 unless it is a Starting Mark. See Rule 43.3(a) when the ground tackle *is* part of the mark. If you foul the rope and it is caught round the keel or rudder you can use your own gear to clear it. See also Rule 55.

52 and **definition – mark.** Even though the mooring rope is not considered part of the mark unless it is a Starting Mark it is still forbidden, under Rule 55, to use the anchor line as a means of avoiding touching the mark.

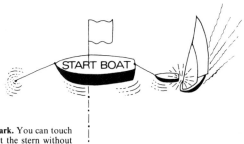

52 and **definition – mark.** You can touch the dinghy tied up at the stern without fear of penalty.

52.1. Touching a Mark. Once you have hit the mark you must do one of three things. Either exonerate yourself under 52.2 (two complete 360° turns – 720°), protest under Rule 68 or exonerate yourself by accepting an Alternative Penalty when laid down in the sailing instruction. See IYRU Case 120.

190

165

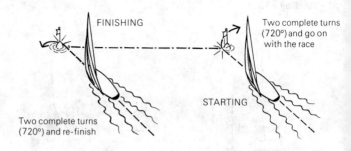

Rule 52.1(a). If you hit a Starting Mark you must complete your exoneration as soon as possible. But if you hit a Finishing Mark you must complete your exoneration before you Finish again.

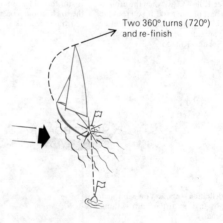

52.1(a)(iii). Touching a Mark at the Finishing Line. According to the definition – Racing and Rule 51.1, if this yacht touches the Mark, even after she has crossed the finishing line, she must exonerate herself and does not finish until she crosses the line a second time.

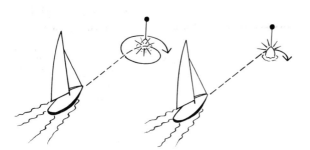

52.2. After touching the mark, both these tracks will correct the error according to this rule.

The key to what has to be done is:
1. The mark has to be rounded or passed according to the sailing instuctions (forgetting about the touching) until the boat is on the new proper course.

2. The penalty of *two* complete turns (720°) which must include two tacks and two gybes must then be completed well clear of any other yachts. Rule 45 says that a yacht that is exonerating herself shall keep clear of other yachts while she does so.

53 – Casting Off, Anchoring, Making Fast and Hauling Out

The whole yacht and its equipment, including the anchor, must be behind the line when kedging before the start.

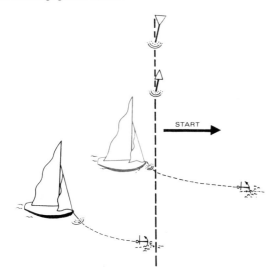

START →

58 – Boarding

If a yacht loses a man overboard she may receive help or assistance from another competitor or spectator yacht as long as no forward progress is made during the recovery operation. See IYRU Case 66.

61 – Clothing and Equipment

In the final paragraph of Appendix 10 a competitor whose weight of wet clothing and equipment exceeds the amount permitted may rearrange the clothing and equipment on the draining rack and repeat the test. This may be interpreted as reweighing the clothing and equipment piece by piece.

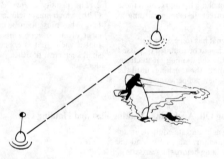

59 – Leaving, crew overboard

When capsizing near the finishing line, a boat may finish with crew members in the water provided they have physical contact with the boat.

62 – Increasing Stability

Crews racing in off-shore yachts equipped with upper and lower lifelines, whether wire or rope, are permitted to have the upper part of their bodies outside the upper lifeline when sitting on the deck facing outboard.

64 – Setting and Sheeting Sails

64.4. Use of Outriggers. Be careful how you fix your jib fairleads so that they do not contravene this Rule, but a hand holding out a sheet is not an outrigger. See IYRU Case 7.

The spinnaker sheet may be led over the mainboom or through a block on the mainboom.

68 – Protests by Yachts

68.2. Informing the Protested yacht. A Protesting yacht must attempt to inform the Protested yacht but it is not mandatory that she succeeds in the attempt. However, you must convince the Protest committee of your attempts. See IYRU Cases 92 and 104.

68.3. Protest flag. The flag must be flown as soon as it is practicable following an incident. A Protest is not lodged until it is written on paper and handed to the race committee. Do not be afraid to fly the Protest flag if you are in any doubt. You may find when you get ashore that it is not necessary to continue with the Protest, in which case you do not have to lodge it. See IYRU Case 47.

68.5. Protest to be in writing. A yacht that is involved in an infringement but which she believes is not her fault must nevertheless lodge a written Protest herself if she wishes to clear herself. See IYRU Case 41 under Rule 52.1.

69 – Requests for Redress

The Race Committee cannot be protested by a yacht. The yacht may seek redress only when she alleges that her finising position has been materially prejudiced. Neither can the Race Committee be expected to know the class rules for each class that is racing. Think of the problems they would have in a multiclass regatta. See IYRU Cases 45, 95 and 119.

70 – Action by Race or Protest Committee

70.4. Measurer's Responsibility. The measurer referred to in this Rule is the measurer appointed specifically for that race or series of races. He is not the measurer of the National authority or the Class measurer (unless of course he has been specially appointed for that race or series of races). See IYRU Case 123.

77 – Appeals

77.1. Right of Appeal. A yacht may appeal only if she has been party to the Protest. If she was not party to the Protest, but affected by the decision and wishing to raise the matter she must seek redress under the terms of Rule 69. See IYRU Case 119.

IYRU Interpretations of the Racing Rules

Part I – Status of the Rules, Fundamental Rules and Definitions

Fundamental Rules

Rendering Assistance

IYRU Case 38. Rendering assistance. Rendering assistance to those in peril is compulsory to those in a position to do so. It does not matter that help may not have been asked for, nor that subsequently it may be shown not to have been needed.

C Fair Sailing

IYRU Case 23. The Fundamental Rule cannot be invoked unless no other rule applies. See also Case 53.

IYRU Case 107. A yacht that deliberately hails 'Starboard' when she is on port tack has not acted correctly and is liable to disqualification.

Accepting Penalties

IYRU Case 2 Accepting a penalty. A yacht which infringes a rule during a race, and continues, can subsequently protest over a later incident.

IYRU Case 138 Retiring promptly. A yacht must retire or exonerate herself by accepting an alternative penalty only when she realises she has infringed a racing rule or sailing instruction, and even then she preserves her rights under Part IV when she continues racing. IYRU Case 135 reinforces.

Definitions

Starting   *IYRU Case 34.* To rank as a starter a boat must either start, or sail about near the line between the preparatory and starting signals. Some scoring systems may include additional boats not in the area at the time.

Finishing   *IYRU Case 102.* The finishing definition cannot be over-ruled by a Sailing Instruction (Rule 3.1). There is no provision for allowing dispensation for other methods of finishing (Rule 51.1(a)).

Tacking   *IYRU Case 32* states that when beating, a yacht has completed her tack when she is heading on a close hauled course, regardless of her movement through the water, or the sheeting of her sails.
            IYRU Case 77. In attempting to pass a mark by shooting head to wind,

a yacht inadvertently passed beyond head to wind and then back again. She was, by definition, in the act of tacking and, having collided with another yacht while doing so, is disqualified under Rule 41.1.

Proper Course
IYRU Case 25. An interpretation of 'proper course' is that there is a logical reason for it and that a yacht sails it with some consistency. When, owing to a difference of opinion as to proper course, two yachts on the same tack converge. Rule 37.1 applies. See also Case 97 below.

Proper Course
IYRU Case 97. A leeward yacht L had no luffing rights over W and based her alteration to a converging course on a temporary spinnaker problem which, she claimed, caused this higher, converging course to be a faster course to the next mark, and hence a 'proper course' for her.

It is correct that new conditions may cause a new proper course to be justifiable, but also that consistency is an essential part of a proper course which cannot be ordinarily or temporarily changed.

In particular a leeward yacht, without luffing rights, is not entitled to use a temporary problem of poor seamanship or sail handling to justify a luff. Since L was aft of 'Mast Abeam', Rule 38.2 applies. See also Case 25 above.

Proper Course
IYRU Case 106 refers to two yachts on converging courses approaching the finishing line. In the absence of W, L would have luffed to finish at right angles to the line, but W wished to sail dead down wind to finish at the starboard end of the finishing line. L did not have luffing rights. However Rule 37 says that when two yachts on the same tack are overlapped then the windward yacht shall keep clear, but that L is limited by Rules 37.3 and 38.2. From the evidence it seemed that L's proper course was correct, and provided that she fulfilled 37.3 and 38.2 she could reasonably assume her proper course, but not luff above it.

Marks and Obstructions
IYRU Case 94. An island begins and ends at the water's edge. When used as a mark, the part below water does not count as a mark. A protruding jetty or rock would be part of the Mark. A yacht going aground below the water's edge would not infringe Rule 52.1(a).

Obstruction
IYRU Case 91. W and L, who are overlapped, are overtaking A, all on the same tack. A ranks as an obstruction to W and L. When either comes within 2 lengths of A Rule 42 starts to apply. W or L can elect to pass their respective sides of A under 42.1(a) and must allow room to the other to do so as well. There is no obligation to hail, though it could be helpful to do so (Rule 42.1(f)).

Part II – Organisation and Management

1. Organising, Conducting and Judging Races

Rule 1.4
IYRU Case 136. Authority for Independent Protest Committee. A race committee may not alter, or refuse to implement, the decision of an independent Protest Committee, including a decision based on a report from an authority qualified to resolve questions of measurement.

Rule 1.5
IYRU Case 131. Right of Appeal. When the decision of a Protest Committee is reversed upon appeal the final standings and the awards must be adjusted accordingly.

Rule 3.1   *IYRU Case 74. Sailing Instructions changing the IYR Rules.* The course instructions of Rule 5 were varied without specific reference as required by Rule 3.1. This omission is incorrect and, in addition, in this case a yacht was materially prejudiced. A Request for Redress under Rule 69 correctly resulted in the race being abandoned and re-sailed. See also IYRU Case 102 on page 170.

Rule 3.2(b)   *IYRU Case 87. Racing after Sunset.* Between sunset and sunrise the Inter-
(xxviii)   national Regulations for Prevention of Collisions at Sea (IRPCS) replace the IYR Rules. Part IV, IYR Definitions are also not applicable to the wordings of the IRPCS. IRPCS Rule 17(a)(i) effectively prevents the 'rac-ing' manoeuvre known as 'luffing', for example. IRPCS phrases such as 'near proximity' have no precise meaning and should be understood in terms of what might, in the circumstances, be seamanlike behaviour. See IYR Appendix 9 – Excerpts from IRPCS.

Rule 3.5   *IYRU Case 75. Sailing Instructions and oral briefing.* The Sailing Instruc-tions cannot require a competitor to attend an oral briefing. He is entitled to expect all necessary information to be contained in the Written Sailing Instructions, possibly with amendments made in accordance with Rule 3.4.

In this case a yacht was materially prejudiced and can take action under 69 (not 68.1 which can only be invoked between two yachts) and there is no requirement therefore to show a protest flag.

Rule 3.5   *IYRU Case 125. Sailing Instructions and Oral briefing.* Before the first race of a series several competitors forget to collect their 'tally boards' before going afloat. The Race Officer permitted this to be corrected by radio.

On the following day this facility was refused when the protesting yacht had sailed three quarters of the course. She was disqualified and appealed. The appeal was dismissed. The Sailing Instruction was mandatory; and in going racing without a tally board, the competitor had contravened the Sailing Instructions.

Rule 4.3   *IYRU Cases 70 and 134. Signals at the start.* Under this rule the timing only of starting signals is governed by the visual signal. There must also be a sound signal but it need not be made at the same moment.

Rule 5.4   *IYRU Case 85. Cancelling – each race is separate.* During the progress of a race the Race Committee may decide under Rule 5 to cancel one or more races in a regatta at its discretion. In this case the RC acted under provisions of 9.1(b) when a mark was missing but cancelled all the races. Subsequent protests to the Jury should only affect those races from whose Competitors protests had been received. Race Committee decisions on other races should stand.

Each race in a multiple regatta is a separate race and should be considered separately.

Rule 5.4   *IYRU Case 140.* A yacht has completed a race when she finishes. When the race is abandoned for those yachts still racing, the Race Committee is bound to consider granting them redress by taking appropriate action.

Rule 5.4c   *IYRU Case 110.* A Race Committee is not entitled to abandon a race on account of a windshift, unless so prescribed in the sailing instructions.

Rule 8   *IYRU Case 134.* A sound signal is obligatory when making a recall signal, as well as a visual signal.

Part III – General Requirements

Rules 18, 20, 21   *IYRU Case 90. Entries, ownerships, helmsman.* Unless specifically stated in the notice of the race or prescribed in the Sailing Instructions the owner, or person in charge, is free to decide who steers a yacht in a race provided Rules 20 and 21 are complied with.

Rule 26   *IYRU Case 139.* Naming a yacht after a commercial establishment when her owner is related in some way to that establishment, is advertising. The definition of advertising is 'an announcement – the act of making generally known'.

Part IV – Right of Way Rules

Section A – Obligations and Penalties

Rule 32   *IYRU Case 51. Avoiding Collisions.* Two yachts in different races were rounding the same mark in opposite directions. Rule 36 applied. P was disqualified. S was also disqualifed for failing to avoid a collision which resulted in serious damage.

Rule 32   *IYRU Case 36. Serious Damage.* In considering whether damage was serious thought should be given to the extent and cost of reinstatement relative to the size of the yacht and whether it was feasible or prudent for her to continue racing; and if so, whether the damage markedly affected her speed and materially prejudiced her finishing position.

Rule 32

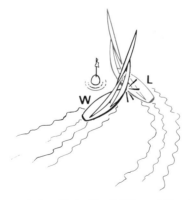

IYRU Case 53. Avoiding Collision and Disqualification. A leeward (L) yacht on port tack tacked without warning and W had no time or warning to avoid a collision and the Protest Committee found this as a fact. W is not required to anticipate that another yacht will infringe a Rule. W is entitled to time to respond. Note that disqualification under Rule 32 is not automatic.

Rule 33   *IYRU Case 141. Contact between Yachts Racing.* An interpretation of 'minor and unavoidable'. The Protest Committee must be satisfied that contact was unavoidable. Only when both of these conditions are fulfilled may yachts be excused for not retiring (or accepting a penalty) or lodging a valid Protest.

Section B – Principal Right of Way Rules and their Limitations

Rule 35   *IYRU Case 10. Close-hauled tacking and keeping clear.* When sailing to windward P bore away to pass astern of S. S, however, tacked. P resumed her course after S had completed her tack. There was no collision. P's alteration in course does not of itself mean that S cannot also do so. In this case Rules 41 and 35 were complied with so no one was at fault.

Rule 35   *IYRU Case 23. Obstructing the right of way yacht.* P bore away to pass under the stern of close-hauled yacht, S. S immediately tacked and the swing of her stern caused P to have to bear away further, so infringing Rule 35 and also 41.1.

Rule 35

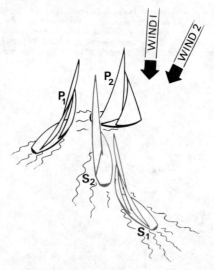

IYRU Case 52. Obstructing after benefiting from a wind-shift. A close-hauled starboard tack yacht luffed to take advantage of a wind shift. P would have been able to cross clear ahead of S before the shift. In this case S was still able to keep clear by bearing away so no rule was infringed. It was S's responsibility under Rule 35 not to prevent P from keeping clear.

Rule 35   *IYRU Case 36. Trying to hit an opposite tack yacht.* Rule 35 always applies and over-rides Rule 36. A right of way starboard tack yacht may not alter course to try to hit a port tack yacht. A starboard tack yacht that hits a port tack yacht without serious damage is not normally penalised.

Rule 35

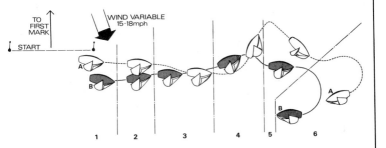

IYRU Case 115. In a typical match racing pre-start manoeuvre one yacht drives another yacht away from the starting line. Yachts A and B reached away from the starting line on port tack. A moving faster passed B and became clear ahead. As A luffed to tack so B luffed with her, preventing A from tacking. A then bore away to gybe but B bore away to leeward of her and prevented her from gybing. Rule 35 applies only to a right of way yacht which B was not, either in position 3 or 4. In position 4 B as windward yacht had to keep clear under Rule 37.1 and A could not tack without infringing 41.1. At position 5 B was leeward yacht and then held rights under Rules 37.1 and 40.

Rule 35

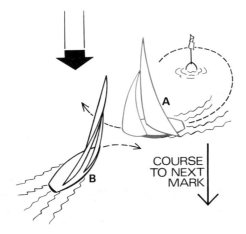

Rule 35

IYRU Case 129. Right of way yacht altering course. Port tack yacht A rounded the windward mark to starboard and immediately gybed onto starboard. Instead of running downwind to the next mark she decided for tactical reasons to reach away at right angles to the course. As she luffed to her new course she came bow to bow with yacht B on port tack still making for the mark. B bore away fast but it was not sufficient and A had to luff sharply as well to avoid the collision. There was no contact. A had no right to luff abruptly into the path of B for whatever reason; tactical desires do not relieve a yacht of her obligations under the Rules. A was disqualified for infringing Rules 35 and 41.2.

Rule 35(b)

IYRU Case 86. Limitations on altering course before the start. Rule 35 does not alter basic rights. Its purpose is to protect a yacht that has to give way from being obstructed in fulfilling this obligation.

In this case B (Behind) was following A (Ahead) during pre-start manoeuvring, including A bearing away and then luffing to assume her proper course to start. During the latter action B touched A's stern and protests under Rule 35. B should have anticipated A's action in luffing to assume proper course and is wrong under Rule 37.2. A did not mislead B.

Rule 36

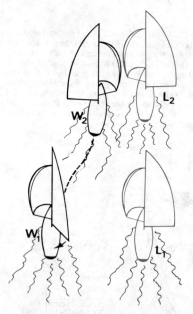

IYRU Case 35. Basic Port/Starboard rule versus Rule 35 (limitations on altering course). W and L were running, overlapped, on port gybe for some time. W gybed onto starboard. She then hailed L and started to luff up slowly. The yachts touched. As a fact it was found that she did not, in this case, infringe Rule 35 and so Rule 36 applies.

Rule 36 also takes precedence, on opposite tacks. S overtakes P from astern. P must keep clear.

Rule 36   *IYRU Case 37. Rounding marks in opposite directions.* Whether by accident or design, in such cases Rule 36 applies. The yachts were not 'about to round the mark on the same side' and so Rule 42 does not apply. See also Case 51 below.

Rule 36   *IYRU Case 51. Rounding marks in opposite directions.* Rule 36 applies (see Case 37). The rules are primarily framed to avoid collisions. In this case P also failed to keep a good lookout and the resulting collision was serious (see Rule 32).

Rule 36   *IYRU Case 45. Three running yachts, one of them on Starboard tack.* S overtook two port tack yachts, which were less than two lengths apart, and intervened between them. Rule 36 applies. There is no question of the port tack yachts being 'obstructions' to S since Rule 42 does not apply. See also Case 45 under Rule 42.3(a).

Rule 36   *IYRU Case 113.* In a straightforward port and starboard case a Protest Committee must inquire carefully into whether the starboard tack yacht did actually bear away to avoid collision, or that there was genuine and reasonable apprehension of collision. If this was so, then the port tack yacht should be disqualified.

Rule 36

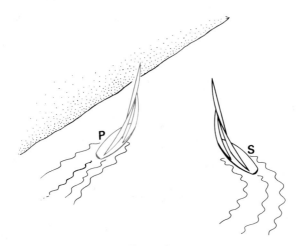

IYRU Case 93. Approaching a continuing obstruction on opposite tacks. P was sailing close-hauled close to, and parallel with, a continuing obstruction. S approached on a collision course. P should keep a good lookout and anticipate such an incident since Rule 36 applies to opposite tack yachts. P must keep clear.

Rule 37.1

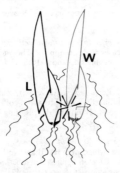

IYRU Case 3. A windward yacht shall keep clear of a leeward yacht. L luffs W correctly until W calls 'Mast Abeam'. Whereupon L bears away suddenly to her proper course. In doing so her tiller extension touches W. W has failed to give L sufficient room and is disqualified.

Rule 37.1

IYRU Case 54. Windward and Leeward yachts at a starting mark. The anti-barging Rule (42.4) and the windward/leeward Rule (37.1) can, and usually do, apply at the same time since they are complementary. Rule of exception only takes precedence when there is conflict.

Rule 37

IYRU Case 11. Overtaking to leeward. When running towards a mark, L steered a course to overtake W and pass to leeward. The moment L established an overlap, W became subject to 37.1. L at the same time became bound by 37.3 and had to allow W room and opportunity to keep clear.

L, now being behind Mast Abeam position was also subject to Rule 38.2 and could not sail above her proper course. In this case, when approaching the mark, L luffed slightly and touched W. It was established that the luff was justified as being an alteration to a new proper course and W was therefore wrong under 37.1.

Rule 37

IYRU Case 46. Overtaking to leeward. On establishing a leeward overlap Rule 37.2 ceases to apply. The windward yacht then becomes bound by 37.1; the leeward yacht by 37.3.

'Ample room and opportunity' to keep clear includes any action such as luffing head to wind if she pleases. If A touches B in so doing then B has not given enough room. B's obligation under 37.3 is not a continuing one, however.

Rule 37

IYRU Case 24. Converging courses before starting. A steady converging course, without luffing, does not infringe Rule 40. Rule 37.1 applies.

Rule 37

IYRU Case 27. Yachts overtaking overlapping yachts clear ahead and attempting to intervene. If the yachts clear ahead are close together Rule 42.3(b) may apply, in which case the yachts clear astern are prohibited from making overlaps on them.

Assuming that there is room for a yacht clear astern to pass between two yachts clear ahead in safety, Rule 37 applies.

When X established an overlap on A she is bound by 37.3; A by 37.1.

When Y established an overlap on D she is bound by 37.1. Y has no right of way between C and D.

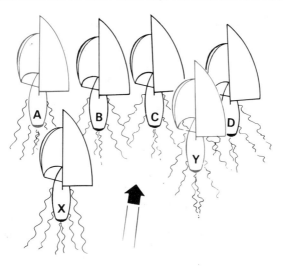

Rule 37

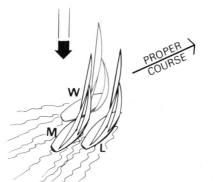

IYRU Case 48. Luffing rights – three overlapping yachts. In this case the yachts were fairly level at one stage, M having luffing rights over W, and L having luffing rights over W and M. Later W drew ahead and bore away somewhat, to go for the mark, touching M, with her stern to M's bow.

It was obvious that M had lost her luffing rights over W at this stage but there was doubt whether L had still retained her luffing rights. W did not hail 'Mast Abeam'.

M was not entitled to luff W. Therefore L was entitled however to continue to sail above her proper course, since there was doubt about her right to luff W, and M had to respond, as intervening yacht, and to keep clear of L under 37.1.

W infringed 37.1 by failing to keep clear and was disqualifed. See also Case 48 under Rule 38.2(e).

Rule 37

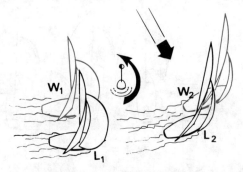

IYRU Case 50. When a mark has been 'passed'. W and L were passing a leeward mark. L gave W adequate room but W was slow in rounding the mark and sheeting in her boom. The Protest Committee found as a fact that W did not round the mark and come up to a proper course as soon as she could do so and there was contact.

It was clear that W and L had passed the mark and that there was no reason for W to sail below her proper course. Rule 42 had ceased to apply. Basic Rule 37.1 applied. W was disqualified.

Rule 37.1   *IYRU Case 116.* Immediately before a start W was dead in the water with sails flapping. L, approaching from leeward, established an overlap and hailed 'Leeward boat'. W took no evasive action until after L had borne away. No contact was made. W clear ahead need not anticipate her obligation to keep clear before being overlapped to leeward from clear astern. Neither yacht was penalised as no rule was infringed.

Rule 37.1   *IYRU Case 114.* In a situation where there are intervening windward yachts being prevented from luffing clear of a leeward yacht, the intervening yachts must do all they can to persuade the windward yacht to keep clear either by luffing or hailing or both.

Rule 37.2   *IYRU Case 68. Overtaking at a continuing obstruction.* A line of running starboard tack boats were sailing one behind the other close to and parallel with a continuing obstruction, the shore.

Yachts clear astern are required, under Rule 37.2, to keep clear of yachts clear ahead.

The leading yacht now gybes on to port but Rule 36 is overridden because they are all subject to the rule of exception, 42, since they are passing an obstruction on the same side. The gybe therefore makes no difference to the terms 'clear ahead' and 'clear astern' which apply here to yachts on opposite tacks. Rule 42.2(a) therefore applies and yachts clear astern must still keep clear.

Rule 37   *IYRU Case 132.* When a yacht has completed her rounding of a mark, Rule 42 ceases to apply and basic rules govern thereafter.

Rule 38   *IYRU Case 58. Starting to tack – limits and intentions.* Two yachts are sailing close-hauled; L, to leeward and ahead, can tack without infringing Rule 41 but, forgetting this she starts to do so. W hails and L returns to her close-hauled course fast. The yachts touched however.

The Protest Committee found as a fact that at no time did L pass through head-to-wind. Therefore, in spite of her admitted original intention to tack, she correctly used her right to luff under Rule 38. W should have kept clear under Rule 37.1. See also IYRU Case 106 under Definition of Proper Course.

Rule 38.2(a)
and 38.2(c)

IYRU Case 101. Hailing for 'Mast Abeam'. Cases of doubt. Normal station. Decisions in this Appeal include: A hail which is not heard is inadequate and must be repeated. In a case of doubt that 'Mast Abeam' position had been reached, L has the right to luff as she pleases and Rule 37.1 applies. But once 'Mast Abeam' has been called she may luff no more. If there was doubt about the call, she must Protest. 'Normal station' can vary, even among yachts of the same class.

Rule 38.2(c)

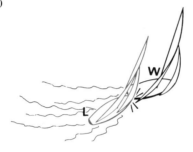

IYRU Case 99. 'Mast Abeam' – a case of doubt. W overtook L at nearly twice her speed. L luffed and W responded. At 'Mast Abeam' W stopped responding but L continued to luff and there was contact in such a position that it was obvious W was ahead of 'Mast Abeam'. Rule 38.2(a) therefore applies. Rule 38.2(c) only applies in cases of doubt.

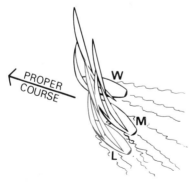

Rule 38

IYRU Case 4. Luffing rights with three yachts. L correctly luffs M and both yachts converge on W who was sailing faster and had reached 'Mast Abeam' by the time they were two lengths apart. There was no hail.
L now had no right to luff under Rule 38.2(a) and was required to turn back to her proper course. However, L continued to luff and M fouled W. W and M should have called for 'water' under Rule 42.1(a). W should have protested against L. See also Case 4 under Rule 42.1(a).

Rule 38.2(e) *IYRU Case 48. Luffing rights – three yachts.* Luffing rights include the right to sail above a proper course. When 'Mast Abeam' position is reached, the leeward yachts must return to a proper course but, if there is doubt, W is not entitled to bear away. She is subject to Rule 37.1, and must also respond under Rule 38.2(e) to a luff from an intervening yacht which has no luffing rights over her, but which is herself required under Rule 37.1 to keep clear of a leeward yacht. See also Case 48 under Rule 37.

Rule 40

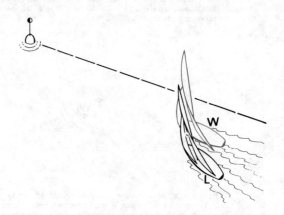

IYRU Case 24. Converging courses before the start. During pre-start manoeuvring L reached a position to leeward and astern of W but was sailing faster. L then sailed a steady converging course on W, gaining an overlap to leeward in the process. The Protest Committee found as a fact that W had ample room and opportunity to keep clear. L did not luff and so Rule 40 did not apply. There was contact and W was disqualified under Rule 37.1.

Rule 41 *IYRU Case 32. Definition of 'Tacking'.* A yacht completes her tack when she reaches the new close-hauled course. Movement through the water and sail sheeting are irrelevant.

Rule 41 *IYRU Case 23. Tacking too close.* P bore away to pass astern of S, but S immediately tacked and thereby caused P to alter course further to avoid her. S infringed Rule 41.1 (and also Rule 35).

Rule 41 *IYRU Case 53. 'Anticipation' and 'Time to respond'.* L, on port tack, tacked without warning on to starboard and hit W immediately after her tack was completed. Even though, in the circumstances, W knew that L was about to tack for the mark, she did not have to anticipate that she would have to give way. She only had to start to take action when L's tack was complete. As with many other rules, time for response is allowed which starts only after the moment right-of-way is actually establised.

Rule 41 *IYRU Case 93. Close handed on opposite tacks near an obstruction.* A port tack close-hauled yacht which is sailing close to leeward of an obstruction must be prepared to avoid a starboard tack yacht which has satisfied Rule 41 and is approaching on a collision course.

Section C – Marks, obstructions and exceptions

Rule 42.1   *IYRU Case 133.* At a mark, when room is made available to a yacht that has no right to it, she may, at her own risk, take advantage of the room so given.

Rule 42.1(a)   *IYRU Case 4. Luffing rights with three yachts.* L, who has luffing rights over M. luffs M until she collides with W. L and M have no luffing rights over W at this point who has drawn ahead of 'Mast Abeam', though no hail was given.
When a collision seemed imminent. M should have called for 'Water' on L under Rule 42.1(a).

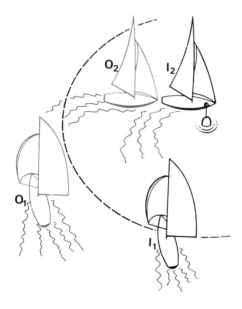

IYRU Case 5. Clear ahead and clear astern at mark. Outside yacht (O) gybed from port to starboard when level with a starboard hand mark but several lengths to the side of it. The inside yacht (I) was on port tack, but clear astern just before O's gybe, but was within two lengths of the mark. O must now keep clear of I, even when I gybed and became clear ahead of O during the rounding. 37.2 is supplemental to 42.

Rule 42.1(a)

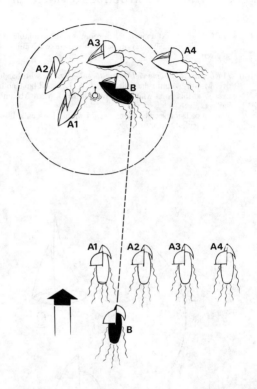

IYRU Case 127. Four yachts in line abreast are running towards a mark on starboard. A fifth yacht B is just clear astern of the line of four. The two inside yachts A1 and A2 gybe on to starboard and round the mark to port satisfactorily. The outer two yachts A3 and A4 still lie outside the two length circle as they start their gybe, and B gybes inside them, now within the two length circle. By Rule 42.3(a)(ii) B is entitled to room around the mark under Rule 42.1(a).

Rule 42.1(a) *IYRU Case 20. Another yacht racing is an obstruction.* W. and L, overlapping, close-hauled on port tack approach S, close-hauled on starboard tack. Normally W must tack if L calls. But in this case S was not an obstruction to L so L could not ask W to tack. W can ask L for room to bear away to pass astern of S. IYRU Case 112 below also refers.

Rule 42.1(a) *IYRU Case 112.* Two yachts, PL and PW, are broad reaching in a lot of wind on port tack. They are on a collision course with yacht S which is beating to windward on starboard tack, S is an obstruction to PW under 42.1(a) who required room from PL to avoid a collision. There was contact

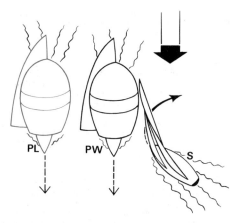

of rigging between S and PW. Rule 36 required the port tack yacht to keep clear but PW was unable to, because PL did not give sufficient room. No hail was required by PW under 34.2. She is only required to hail if she makes an alteration of course which was unforeseen. This clearly was not the case as both port gybe yachts were aware of yacht S. PL was disqualified.

Rule 42.1(a)

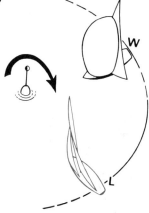

IYRU Case 21. Overlaps on widely differing courses. L, on starboard tack, approached a starboard hand mark close-hauled. W approached from almost directly upwind and called for room to round the mark inside L. At all material times W had an overlap on L under the definition and was therefore entitled to room under Rule 42.1(a).

Rule 42.1(a)   *IYRU Case 40. An interpretation of 'room'.* 'Room' means, enough space to enable the inside boat, in the prevailing conditions and handled in a seamanlike manner, to pass in safety between the object and the outside boat.

Rule 42.1(a)   *IYRU Case 50. When a mark is 'passed'.* W and L were overlapped at a mark. L gave W adequate room. The Protest Committee found as a fact that W was unnecessarily slow in luffing up, and disqualified W after contact with L under 37.1. When adequate room at a mark has been given under 42.1(a) the basic rules apply again.

Rule 42.1(a)   *IYRU Case 76. Room at an obstruction. New overlap starts after tacking.* Two overlapping yachts were close-hauled. Both tacked and a new overlap began at that point which was more than two lengths from an obstruction. The new outside yacht was obliged to give the inside yacht room under Rule 42.1(a).

Rule 42.1(e)   *IYRU Case 62. After the mark – turning to a proper course.* An inside yacht without luffing rights, having been given room to round a mark, must assume her new proper course, under Rule 38.2, as soon as she is able to do so. If bearing away to a proper course includes a need to gybe. then she must gybe as required in 42.1(e). Proper course changes when the inside boat gets about halfway past the mark. See also definition of Proper Course.

Rule 42.1(f)   *IYRU Case 91. Hailing.* There is no obligation to hail for room at a mark or obstruction. A yacht need take no such action though a hail could be helpful in supporting a claim if a protest followed.

Rule 42.2(a)   *IYRU Case 68. Anticipation during rounding or passing marks or obstructions.* A line of yachts, each clear astern of the next ahead, are passing a continuous obstruction, the shore line. Even though a yacht ahead gybes on to port, a starboard tack yacht clear astern still has to keep clear in anticipation of the rounding or passing manoeuvre since Rule 42 applies. (Here the clause is 42.2(a).

Rule 42.2(a)

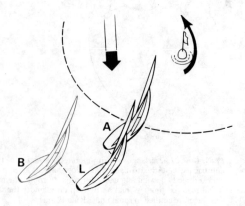

IYRU Case 59. Overtaking when about to round a mark. When A came within two lengths of the mark, L had a leeward overlap on A; B had a windward overlap on L. L was therefore not an 'intervening yacht' B was, however, overhauling A and L fast, but had no rights to room on A's windward side.

B is entitled to room between A and L under 42.1(a) but must keep clear of A under 42.2(a).

Rule 42.2(c)

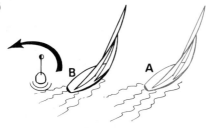

IYRU Case 26. Yacht clear ahead – tacking round a mark. Approaching a windward mark close-hauled, A is clear ahead but to leeward of B. A cannot tack if she thereby infringes Rule 41. B, however, can hold her course to prevent A tacking. Rule 42.2(c) governs the situation.

Rule 42.3(a)   *IYRU Case 45. Opposite tacks – overtaking.* W and L were running on port tack. S overtakes first L and then W and intervenes between them. S has right of way under Rule 36 over both port tack yachts, consequently W does not rank as an obstruction to S and Rule 42.3(a) does not apply between S and L.

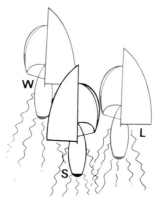

Rule 42.3(a) and (b) *IYRU Case 67. Establishing an overlap at a continuous obstruction.* W and L were running overlapped on the same gybe towards the finish, almost two lengths apart. M overtook and intervened, establishing overlaps on both yachts. There was no contact but W protested that M was not entitled to room.

L and W were within two lengths of each other and L was an obstruction with respect to the other two. L was a continuing obstruction to W and, under Rule 42.3(b), M established a legal overlap which was shown by there being no contact thereafter.

Rule 42.3(b) *IYRU Case 27. Rules for establishing overlaps on continuous obstructions – other yachts.* See also Case 27 under Rule 37 which governs cases where a yacht overhauls a line of yachts abreast and tries to intervene. The yachts ahead form continuing obstructions and so the yacht clear astern may not try to establish an overlap under Rule 43.3(b) unless there is room to do so and to pass right through in safety (i.e. without touching either yacht ahead).

Rule 42.3(b) *IYRU Case 69. Establishing overlaps on continuous obstructions – the shore line.* The rule is that no attempt to establish an overlap may be made unless the yacht can do so and pass in safety. 'Safety' means – without touching the yacht ahead or running aground.

When a successful overlap is established, the overtaking yacht can claim room under Rule 42.1(a) and cannot be luffed into the obstruction.

Rule 42.4 *IYRU Case 54. Anti-barging rule complements Rule 37.* Rule 42.4 is a rule of exception to the basic rule in a special situation, but this does not mean that the basic rule is totally overridden or in abeyance. It is only when there is conflict that the rule of exception takes precedence. In the case of barging at the start the basic rule is usually complementary to Rule 42.4.

Rule 43 *IYRU Case 80. The amount of room required when tacking at an obstruction.* After a reply of 'You Tack' to L's hail on approaching an obstruction, L tacked and was able to avoid W, but she cannot claim that her 'loss of distance' in doing so entitles her to succeed in a protest against W.

Rule 43 *IYRU Case 93. Close-hauled on opposite tacks near a continuing obstruction.* A close-hauled port tack yacht which is sailing close to, and parallel with, a continuing obstruction, must be prepared for a starboard tack yacht approaching on a collision course and to take early avoiding action. Rule 43 does not apply since they are on opposite tacks.

Rule 43.1 *IYRU Case 117.* Two yachts approaching the shore on starboard tack. The leeward yacht a length ahead and a length-and-a-half to leeward. The leeward yacht hails but is not heard. W does not respond but L tacks, tries to bear away underneath the stern of W but hits her several feet forward of the transom. On this occasion it seems that the hail was not adequate and a second louder hail should have been made. L was disqualified under Rule 36.

Rule 43.2(a) *IYRU Case 6. Responding to a hail to tack at an obstruction.* W and L, close-hauled and overlapped on port tack, were approached by S, close-hauled on starboard tack. S hailed for water; L hailed W to avoid S but obtained no response to three hails. S bore away to avoid a collision with L. S protested L. W retired.

The Appeals Committee ruled that L did enough to satisfy her obligations. She was entitled to expect W to respond. She was not obliged to bear away astern of S or to anticipate W's failure to comply with Rule 43.2(a).

Rule 44   *IYRU Case 81. Rights of a premature starter.* W and L were overlapped at the start, sailing close-hauled. Both were premature starters though W was unaware of this fact. W's rights under Rule 44.2 were confined to those conferred by Rule 35 until the moment L bore away to return and re-start, at which moment she acquired full rights in respect of L, not knowing she was a premature starter and not attempting to re-start. L, in bearing away to re-start, was therefore required to keep clear of W under 44.1(a). In this case her tiller touched W and so she was disqualified.

Part V – Other Sailing Rules

Rule 50   *IYRU Case 34. Ranking as a starter.* Shortly before the starting signal was made, the race was postponed, but this did not prevent several yachts starting and sailing the course. The new race was started but the other yachts did not return. They were recorded as not having started since they were not in the vicinity of the starting line between five minute and starting guns.

Rule 50   *IYRU Case 111. Ranking as a Starter.* Several yachts were on the course side of the line at the starting gun. Some were half a mile away. The Race Officer did not fire a second gun as he was required to do to signify individual recalls, nor was the class flag flown at the 'dip'. The nearest yacht to the line, A, some 20 yards from the line, thought she was in the clear and sailed the race from which she was subsequently disqualifed. However, she did rank as a starter under Rule 50, being in the vicinity of the line. And she was therefore subject to Rule 8.1 (Recalls) and 51.1(a) and (b) Sailing the Course and should be granted some redress.

Rule 51.1(a)   *IYRU Case 102. Finishing instructions.* The finishing definition cannot be overruled by a Sailing Instruction. There is no provision for allowing dispensation for other methods of finishing.

Rule 51

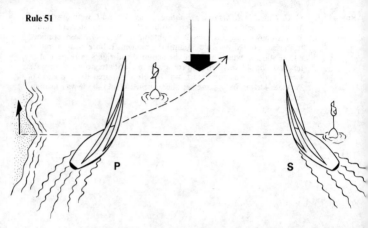

IYRU Case 124. Limit marks on the finishing line. The inner limit mark was well on the post-finish side of the line. P crossed the line ahead of S, but well shorewards of the inner limit mark. Subsequently she passed the inner limit mark, leaving it to port. S, at the other end of the line, crossed the finishing line and left the outer limit mark to starboard. S requested redress saying that the Race Officer had finished P before she had rounded the inner limit mark and therefore before she had completed the course.

The Protest Committee refused the request for redress and referred its decision for confirmation. This was forthcoming. A limit mark that lies on the post-finish side of a finishing line does not rank as a mark.

Rule 52.1 *IYRU Case 41. Wrongfully compelled to touch a mark.* When wrongfully forced to touch a mark it is not enough to hoist a protest flag or expect the other yacht to retire. A written protest must be lodged in order to protect the case of the injured yacht. Rule 52.1 is the only rule that requires a yacht to retire when she fails to comply with the mandatory requirements of that Rule and Protest, or to exonerate herself as provided by Rule 52.2.

Rule 52.1 *IYRU Case 56. Wrongfully compelled to touch a mark – incorrect start.* A yacht runs over a starting mark which sinks and re-surfaces, touching another yacht on its pre-start side. Thus the second yacht not only touched the mark but failed to start correctly since she passed the mark on the incorrect side. She has to return, re-start correctly or exonerate herself and protest the other yacht. Without the protest the Race Committee cannot consider redress under Rule 69.

IYRU Case 120. Touching a mark. Two yachts involved in a collision and one of them hit the finishing mark. This latter yacht neither protested nor exonerated herself and was disqualified. When a mark is touched, the yacht which makes this infringement must either protest under Rule 68 or exonerate herself.

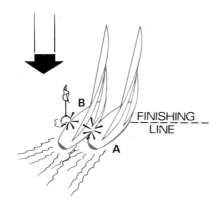

Rules 53, 55   *IYRU Case 94. Hauling out on an island also used as a turning mark.* Rules 53 and 55, when they apply, overrule the provisions of Rule 52.

Rule 60   *IYRU Case 66. Outside assistance etcetera.* A yacht lost a man overboard but took some time lowering spinnaker and preparing to recover him (Rule 59). Meanwhile a spectator boat picked up the man and returned him aboard the yacht. This did not contravene Rule 60 because of the specific exception to receiving outside assistance contained therein.

Rule 64.4

IYRU Case 7. Definition of 'outrigger'. An outrigger is defined as a 'fitting'. the crew's hand is not a 'fitting' and can therefore be used to hold a sheet outboard.

Part VI – Protests, Penalties and Appeals

Rule 68.2   *IYRU Case 92. Informing a yacht protested against.* It is mandatory that a protesting yacht shall try to inform the yacht protested against that a protest will be lodged, but failure to succeed does not invalidate the protest. A claim by the protested yacht that she did not know she was being protested against is not a ground for not hearing the protest.

Rule 68.2   *IYRU Case 104. Informing a yacht protested against.* An attempt to inform is mandatory. It is not mandatory to succeed.

When Appendix 3 (720° turns) applies it is required that the yacht is informed by hail and by protest flag. The hail is the most important and should be immediate, otherwise the protested yacht is unable to take advantage of the opportunity to exonerate herself.

When the Race Committee is satisfied that a yacht has failed to 'try to inform' the protest shall not be heard, but a yacht cannot be disqualified for this reason.

Rule 68.3   *IYRU Case 47. Failure to display a protest flag.* A yacht which has knowledge of the facts of an incident, but is not certain of the rules, must nevertheless first show a protest flag, which can be withdrawn later if it appears that no infringement took place.

Rule 68.6   *IYRU Case 142.* Although this rule does allow the Protest Committee to extend the time limit for lodging protests it does not relieve the witness of an incident from ascertaining promptly whether or not a protest had been lodged.

Rule 69   *IYRU Case 74. Seeking redress from a Race Committee.* In a case where the sailing instructions for altering course were not correctly referred to as required under Rule 3.1 it was clear that a yacht's chances of winning were prejudiced. Accordingly a decision to abandon and re-sail under Rule 69 was appropriate.

Rule 69   *IYRU Case 95. Seeking redress – criteria.* In this case the Race Committee found as a fact that no yachts were materially prejudiced, or that the race was unfair. A yacht may not protest against the Race Committee, but she may seek redress only if her finishing position has been prejudiced.

Rule 70.2(b)   *IYRU Case 18. A late protest.* After a race it came to the notice of the Race Committee that a yacht had touched a starting line mark and neglected to take appropriate action. In spite of the fact that Declarations were not required, the Race Committee may take action under Rule 70.2(b).

Rule 70.4   *IYRU Case 123. Measurer's Responsibility.* Two IOR rated yachts in a summer long series. One yacht, yacht A, was found to have sailed the series with an incorrect rating certificate. B requested redress under Rule 69. It was subsequently found by the national rating authority that there was an error in the rating certificate dating from the first hull measurement some years back. The protest committee found that the owner of yacht A was not responsible for the error and that he had not infringed Rule 19. The Protest Committee decided that the Race Committee was not responsible for the error and therefore yacht B was not entitled to redress under Rule 69. The Protest could not be heard under Rule 70.4 because no measurer had been appointed for that series. Retrospective action for faulty rating certificates relating to yachts in a series would mean that no series could be concluded, which is simply not acceptable.

Rule 71.1   *IYRU Case 90. No disqualification without a hearing.* The Race Committee considered, incorrectly, that a yacht had not been entered in the manner prescribed, and therefore decided she was a non-starter, and was not awarded finishing points. She should not have been penalised without a hearing.

Rule 74.1   *IYRU Case 77. Decisions based on facts.* In a Protest resulting from contact between yachts, a Race Committee must find the relevant facts and make a decision based on them.